SHORTCUTS
for Teachers

Strategies for Reducing Classroom Workload

Jean Enk   Meg Hendricks

A Learning Handbook™

Fearon Teacher Aids
a division of

PITMAN LEARNING, INC.

Belmont, California

Editorial director: Roberta Suid
Editor: Buff Bradley
Production editor: Gustavo Medina
Design manager: Eleanor Mennick
Designer: Stan Tusan
Cover designer: Jim M'Guinness

Library of Congress Catalog Card Number: 81-81392
Printed in the United States of America

ISBN-0-8224-6373-3

1. 9 8 7 6 5 4 3

Contents

INTRODUCTION

No one needs to remind classroom teachers that they have overwhelming workloads. No one needs to point out to them that much of what they do every day *isn't* teaching. But someone should help teachers find ways to lighten those workloads; ways to get nonteaching tasks done more quickly and efficiently; ways to enlist the help of others; ways to streamline record-keeping, classroom management, discipline, planning, filing, and the myriad other chores that are part of every classroom; ways to spend less time and effort picking up, cleaning up, making up, following up, and more time *teaching*.

This book offers help in the form of "Shortcuts," strategies for shrinking, delegating, and in some cases eliminating various time-consuming, classroom-related tasks. These Shortcuts are not theoretical; they've emerged from more than forty years of teaching experience. They've been tested day in, day out, by the authors and their colleagues. These Shortcuts really work.

In no sense does using any of the Shortcuts interfere with maintaining high professional standards. It is perfectly possible to relieve yourself of extra work without sacrificing your commitment to giving students your best. To succeed in lightening your load, however, you must be willing to give up being involved in absolutely everything that happens in your classroom. That giving up isn't always easy, since many teachers feel it means losing touch— and losing control. If you are ready and willing to surrender some of your work, then you must also be able to recognize the opportunities for doing so when and where they appear.

In its eight chapters, *Shortcuts for Teachers* spots dozens of those opportunities for you and gives specific, helpful suggestions on everything from arranging your room, to enlisting volunteers, to establishing a system of discipline. And while each chapter addresses one major subject, it's clear there are no such neat divisions among the tasks necessary to keep a classroom going. Discipline and record-keeping obviously overlap; so do planning and paperwork; so do management and materials. Then again, planning and record-keeping overlap, as do testing and management and paperwork, and so on. All this is simply to say it's best if you read *Shortcuts for Teachers* once through entirely before you put any of the Shortcuts into effect. Get an overview of what the book is all about, get a feel for the content, see how your own circumstances fit or don't fit with what's suggested here. Then pick a few of the Shortcuts that seem most appropriate to you and try them out.

Shortcuts aren't written in stone, and you may find you need to change various ones somewhat to suit your needs. Make any changes you wish. Shortcuts are not only how-to's; they also are intended to be consciousness-raisers, strategies that get you to *think* as well as to *do*. Once you start using the Shortcuts you should also start asking yourself, "Is this activity (or material or piece of equipment) really necessary to learning? Can I do this job more efficiently and easily? Should someone else be doing this job for me? How can I make this material permanent and avoid having to remake it? Can I adapt this material or activity for other purposes?" The more you ask yourself these kinds of questions, the closer you move toward the essential work of a teacher—teaching children, not fussing with a million other details.

Begin implementing Shortcuts slowly, and proceed with a plan. Focus on that part of your workload you most want to pare down, record-keeping, for instance. Examine your record-keeping responsibilities, read all the record-keeping Shortcuts carefully and critically, and start with one or two that seem as if they'll work for you. When those Shortcuts are adopted comfortably into your over-all teaching scheme, try a few more and make changes where appropriate. After you've cut your record-keeping time down to size, work on another area that could use improvement. It may take you a full school year, or more, to incorporate a full array of Shortcuts into your classroom routine. But from the moment you put the first one into effect, you'll find yourself with more time to teach at school, and more time to yourself after school, than you had before.

ROOM
ENVIRONMENT

A place where teachers and students come together is an important place, important because of the learning that happens there. But too often the physical makeup of the classroom becomes an end in itself. Some educators evaluate teachers by evaluating their classrooms. Some teachers treat their rooms as status symbols and spend long hours beautifying them to "keep up with the Joneses" across the hall.

Instead of worrying about the beauty of their classrooms, teachers would do well to focus on the utility of those rooms. The teacher's efforts should be to ensure that the room is a pleasant, stimulating, and functional learning place. What goes on the walls, how desks are arranged, how traffic will flow, where materials are stored, what equipment is present, are all decisions about the educational quality of the environment. Making and acting upon these decisions can and should be shared responsibilities—the teacher doesn't have to do all the work alone.

BULLETIN BOARDS

Walk down any school hallway before, after, and sometimes even during school hours, especially at the beginning of each month, and you'll likely see teachers and their aides busily at work on bulletin boards. It is not unusual for some teachers to spend 20 hours a month or more on bulletin boards even though some studies have shown that:

- [ ] Teacher-made displays are not as significant to children as things they have done themselves.
- [ ] "Teaching" bulletin boards don't necessarily teach.
- [ ] Calendar bulletin boards may be a waste of teacher and student time as well as wall space, especially in the upper grades.
- [ ] Achievement boards, such as "Spell Your Way to the Top Cloud," may undermine the confidence of the very children who most need to be motivated.
- [ ] Bulletin boards that use many bright colors, large cartoon figures, and the like, may distract children and actually hinder learning.
- [ ] There is nothing wrong with a blank bulletin board, especially one that is backed by a pleasing nonintrusive material.

There are ways to make monthly bulletin boards tasks easier and less time-consuming, but first the teacher should ponder these questions:

- [ ] Do I work in a school where the principal tends to judge teacher competency in terms of pretty boards with straight borders and where district directives imply, "We'll be checking for evidence of plenty of after-hours effort?"
- [ ] Do I spend a lot of time on my bulletin boards because I always have or because I like the strokes I get from others? Or am I afraid not to because everyone else does, and I don't want to appear lacking in comparison?
- [ ] Do I consider bulletin boards to be fine motivational teaching tools?

☐ Do I want to provide young lives with a spot of beauty that may not be available elsewhere in the environment?

Obviously the answers to these questions reflect how a teacher uses bulletin boards. If the principal and other administrators place great stock in how classroom wall space is used, it would be foolhardy to disregard their wishes. But if a teacher spends untold hours of precious time only out of habit or simply because other teachers do it, that teacher needs to reevaluate.

Further questions teachers ought to mull over concern how they see themselves professionally:

☐ Am I a seasoned, confident, tenured professional who can weigh the variables, make intelligent choices, and stand up to outside pressures if necessary?

☐ Am I a beginning teacher, long-term substitute, temporary, or probationary teacher whose future is still in the hands of others and who needs to be concerned about making good impressions?

☐ Am I an older teacher concerned about maintaining the impression that I can do the job as well as the youngsters and that I am not "sliding into retirement"?

The way a teacher views his or her place in the profession will influence use of time, independence of choices, and expenditure of effort on various tasks.

✂ *SHORTCUTS*

DO IT ONCE

Back all boards with a neutral color such as black, white, beige, or brown and frame them with a contrasting yarn stapled into place. If the board is new or nicely painted, leave it as is. Use nonfading butcher paper, cloth, wallpaper or wrapping paper—something that will last—then leave the boards that way for the entire year.

If some of the boards are covered with simple, repeating designs like those found on inexpensive wrapping paper or wallpaper remnants, then those boards can be left empty at various times. Such boards are not distracting, yet they help to make the room cheerful and inviting.

CUT OUT CUT-OUTS

Cutting out letters for captions is a ridiculous use of teacher or aide time. Print labels on tagboard or colored strips. If life is not livable without individual letters, invest in reuseable commercial ones.

Making cute seasonal cut-outs to go on a calendar is another waste of time. Bulletin board calendars could be eliminated completely since their teaching value is questionable. There are more effective ways of teaching the passage in terms of days and months. But if a calendar seems essential, buy or make a laminated one, write on it, erase it, and use it over and over again.

If achievement boards such as "Fly to the Moon" really seem necessary and you can't find a quicker, simpler way of recording growth, then at least have the students cut out their own figures or markers during one of those times when a few minutes' filler is needed. Simple geometric shapes made with a paper cutter are fast and easy to make.

USE COMMERCIAL POSTERS

Collect the commercial posters that are distributed at school (health, safety, famous men and women, and so on). Assign a student or a group of students to be in charge of displaying these posters in a special place, in a special way, for the whole year. That special way might be off-center and deliberately angled to reduce a teacher's urge to straighten something a child has put up.

KEEP IT SIMPLE, MAKE IT VERSATILE

Large tagboard disks or paper plates, painted with enamel or laminated and arranged in a variety of ways, provide endless possibilities for quick bulletin boards. They can be balloons, suns and moons, scoops of ice cream, backgrounds for snapshots, you name it. Keep the disks up on the bulletin board all year; rearrange them quickly once a month.

PUT THE KIDS IN CHARGE

The preceding Shortcuts are modifications of what is common practice in classrooms now. But in order to take the bulletin board monkey off your back permanently and at the same time do good things with and for students, consider giving the children the responsibility for keeping the classroom interesting and beautiful.

Begin by assigning each student a space on the boards or walls that is hers or his alone. Use hall space outside the classroom if you have and need it. If it is impossible to find a spot for all the students at one time, assign space on a rotating basis. Remember, the fewer rotations, the less paperwork is necessary to keep track of whose turn is when.

Discuss with the class how important each contribution will be, how carefully and thoughtfully it ought to be executed, and how regularly the displays should be changed. We have found that even kindergarten children accept this responsibility with enthusiasm, and even at that early age they begin to plan ahead by asking that projects be saved to be used later on their own bulletin board spaces.

Providing time and materials for making monthly changes in bulletin boards takes surprisingly little teacher preparation or planning if this work is woven smoothly into the routine of the classroom. Once a month, set aside two one-hour classroom periods and one hour of teacher or aide time outside of class. Use one of the classroom hours for an art project and one for the written narrative; use the hour of teacher/aide time to pin up or supervise the students as they pin up the finished work.

Keep the materials for art projects very simple. You should provide enough variety to keep students interested, yet use materials that are easily boxed and kept ready for use once a month and that can be distributed and collected without a lot of fuss. A box or two of colored pens, colored pencils, scraps of colored paper, graph paper, crayons, and colored chalk are trouble free and quick.

Subject matter for the bulletin boards might reflect a particular area of study, a field trip, or a classroom project; or you can give students the freedom to display whatever they like. The artwork and the written work might complement each other, or they may be unrelated. One month, for example, students might write about a field trip and illustrate the narratives with drawings, paintings, or sculptures of what they saw on the trip. Another month you could give students the choice of what to display—favorite poems, stories, artwork, whatever. Students who don't yet write will, of course, need to dictate their stories to aides, parent volunteers, or cross-age tutors, who will write the stories in yellow marking pen or chalk. Then the children can copy or trace over the stories and display them. All students should be encouraged to do their very best. Written work should be neat and easy to read. The teacher can check first drafts and mark errors; then the students use black marking pens to redo their work for display.

Our experience has been that the more varied these monthly projects, the more interest they generate among the students in the room and from students in the rest of the school. One of the extra benefits of this method of using bulletin boards is that, when given the opportunity to put up what they want in their spaces, students become more interested in the boards of others as well as their own. It is not unusual for children to ask permission to enter another classroom to read the latest boards. Thus, the chance that some real learning is taking place increases.

FURNITURE ARRANGEMENT

No teacher who has taught even a little while will deny that furniture arrangement affects the way things run in the classroom.

Children sitting at desks in close clusters interact with each other more than those sitting in straight, separated rows facing front. This interaction may help students to learn from each other and may generate cooperation and positive feelings. Small group instructions become easier for the teacher when students sit in clusters. Committee work and a centers plan fit into this pattern nicely. However, more interaction between students usually means more noise and greater likelihood of disruption.

Desks in straight, separated rows facing front provide a "territory" for each child, a space that is his or hers alone. This territory may be very important to children whose homes are overcrowded and who must share almost everything. A desk of one's own and a foot of space on all four sides may make some children feel very good. Also, teachers who present new material in lectures can be certain everyone can see and hear comfortably when all seats face front. There is a united focus on front and center. Movies, filmstrips, and overhead projector presentations too work better with this arrangement. The fact that everyone is facing the teacher is no automatic assurance, however, that learning is going on. Children around the edges and in the back may, in fact, be tuned in to something quite different from what is going on in the front of the classroom.

Where a teacher puts his or her desk also influences learning. A desk in the center of things may allow the teacher to conduct almost all classroom activities behind that desk. A desk in a corner forces a teacher to get out among the troops. Proximity to the teacher seems to have some relationship to amount learned, and there's no way that a row arrangement can put all children equidistant from the teacher.

Research as to the best room arrangement for learning is inconclusive. The age and maturity of the children, the teaching philosophy and style of the teacher, the type and amount of furniture, the size and design of the classroom, and the extent to which audio-visual equipment is used in the curriculum are all variables that influence decisions regarding room arrangement. The only ''musts'' that can be agreed on are that the room should be easy to look at, easy to move around in, and easy to function in.

To be easy to look at, a room should be neat and clean. This requirement takes care of itself if the janitor does a good job and the teacher and children maintain a modicum of neatness and cleanliness without clutter.

To be easy to move around in, a room requires traffic lanes wide enough for two to pass without problems; plenty of room around entrances and exits; and sufficient access to chalkboards, sinks, and centers so that students won't stumble over chairs or other objects.

To be easy to function in, a room requires cupboard doors that can be opened without moving something first, chairs that fit the tables, and audio-visual equipment that is available for use but does not steal valuable operating room when idle. Neither sunlight nor artificial light should shine directly into students' eyes. Because many school districts now require diminished lighting to conserve energy, furniture must be arranged so that good light is available on dark and rainy days.

✂ SHORTCUTS

USE YOUR HEAD,
NOT YOUR BACK

Watch, listen, and think about what happens as teacher and students work their way through each day's curriculum. Ask, ''Could I improve the physical setting of this classroom so that working in it would be easier and more pleasant?'' Having pinpointed a road-block, go for the paper and pencil, or chalk and chalkboard. Draw out a plan for change. It's much easier than moving heavy furniture several times. Deal with flaws in the new plan on paper before you exert one gram of muscular energy.

DO A LITTLE AT A TIME

If clutter is a problem, don't tackle the whole room at one time. Look at one corner or a 5 x 5 foot area. Cast a sharp eye over every inch of that space to inspect it for snarls. Would another bookcase get those books off the floor? Is that box really needed? Whatever jars nerves or sensibilities is a fit subject for reworking. Taken corner by corner, area by area, a big job becomes manageable.

LABEL CHAIRS

To eliminate arguments, number the chairs that go around a particular table. The backs of chairs that go around ''Table One'' should have the numeral ''1'' taped to them. To save time in matching chairs to large and small students, put children's names on the backs with black marking pen. (Ink washes off easily with a little cleanser.)

USE THE AIR SPACE

Think of air space as usable. Listening posts placed on a table take up too much surface area and make the table top unavailable for anything else. Couple that drawback with the inevitable tangle of earphone jack wires and the result is a mess. Consider suspending the listening post from the ceiling, light fixture, whatever, an you'll have table cords that dangle rather than tangle.

Hang a string or wire across the room or down one side. Attach clothespins and you have a ''clothesline'' for wet paintings that would otherwise sit on tables and counters.

MAKE A SCREEN

Not every school has the money to buy permanently mounted wall screens for showing movies, filmstrips, or overhead projector lessons. Don't despair. Keep the wall above the chalkboard clear and project onto it. Under most circumstances, everyone in the class will be able to see pictures focused there. If that's not satisfactory, try turning a wall map over and using that nice white reverse side for a screen.

USE THE FILE CABINETS

File cabinets are a boon for storing many of the tools of the teacher's trade. Their place in a room should be convenient to those who will be using them. Further, don't overlook the possibility of placing a file cabinet so that it serves as a divider setting off a quiet work area or a "thinking place"—handy things to have in a classroom. Also, since display area for children's work is often limited, consider using the sides of the file cabinet for display. File cabinets are child-height, easily cleaned, and large enough to hold several pieces of student work. (For suggestions about setting up an effective filing system, see page 58.)

CUPBOARDS, SHELVES, CLOSETS, TEACHER'S DESK

The amazing amount of materials and equipment necessary for individualized programs can overwhelm the classroom. Often a good lesson does not get taught or a good teaching device does not get used because the teacher simply cannot find it quickly, and hunting through the debris is just plain not worth the trouble. It is not uncommon, particularly in schools receiving additional funds for economically deprived students, to find so many manipulatives, games, visual aids, and other equipment, that some things are still unpacked, unopened, and forgotten in the cupboards. Almost every teacher can be heard to say at least sometime during the school year, "I guess I'd better clean out my closets, there's probably a lot of stuff in there that I don't even know I have."

Using shelves, cupboards, and drawers to the best advantage is an important part of a teacher's job. The immediate convenience of stowing something in whatever place is nearest at hand becomes an inconvenience days later when you can't recall where you put those workbooks, that gameboard, those colored pencils. Your particular habits and preferences will determine finally what goes where. But begin with an overall plan.

✄ *SHORTCUTS*

ORGANIZE CUPBOARDS AND CLOSETS BY SUBJECT

Organize all closed cupboards by academic subject area. For example, one floor-to-ceiling cupboard for science and math, one of similar size for reading and language, and so forth. Then within each subject cupboard use color-coded boxes (paint the fronts with tempera) that are labeled and numbered. This kind of coding enables a teacher to ask a student or an aide to get the yellow box in the reading cupboard with the numeral "3" on it, or the blue box labeled "fraction flash cards." The teacher does not need to get up; the directions are easy to give and carry out. (Math lab boxes available from Creative Publications are inexpensive and have the advantage of being color-coded with labels included.)

DON'T DO IT ALL AT ONCE

Once you decide on a plan, set aside a regular time for dealing with closets and cupboards and get started. Always use the amount of time you've allotted yourself, and quit when the time is up. Do not empty a whole closet at once. Take it one shelf at a time, and if things are really in a mess, take only one section of that shelf at a time. Take everything out that does not belong there and put it where it will eventually belong. Remember to arrange just one area at a time. Don't get caught in the trap of trying to organize all shelves simultaneously. No matter that things will be in a hodgepodge at first; it will all get better soon. Don't try for perfection. Many teachers waste their good energies on things that don't really have to be all that perfect.

USE SPACE WISELY

Place those things used most frequently on lower shelves and those used less often on upper shelves. This approach seems merely common sense, yet many teachers give no thought to such planning when organizing storage spaces. Don't waste cupboard space by devoting an entire shelf to just a few oversized items. Instead, add an intervening shelf and use the space for twice as many smaller items. Find a space for the larger ones under a counter or over a cupboard. Remember that any empty or hollow space is a potential container. Before seeking additional space, however, organize what is already available. Adding space before "redoing" the old is just finding more space to be disorganized in.

Extra space can be found in most ordinary classrooms once a determined and critical eye begins to seek it. For example, adding a shelf between existing shelves may be only a matter of getting the wood, cutting it, and then putting two bracing strips along the side walls to hold it. Put hooks inside the cupboard doors and use the hanging space for anything hangable. There are plastic bags made with reinforced holes for just such a purpose.

ORGANIZE OPEN SHELVES
BY ACTIVITY

Organize all open shelves *by activity* for student convenience. For example, place all spare-time games in one area, reading series in another, leisure time reading books in yet another. Put paper and other often-used materials out where students can get to them, pass them out, and keep them neat. Too often these materials are kept in cupboards; and only the teacher, hoping to exercise more control over waste and misuse, can distribute them. Actually, this is one more task that you should eagerly give up. In our experience, expensive, scarce supplies can be controlled just as easily out in the open.

LET EVERYONE USE YOUR DESK

Open the teacher's desk for the use of everyone in the classroom. (Keep one drawer out-of-bounds if you need a private place.) A teacher who does all the staple-removing, paper-punching, notice-writing, and paper clip-getting is wasting good teaching time and energy. To be sure, students don't need to get to purses, grade books, or lunch money, so an inaccessible place such as a file drawer or locked closet is probably necessary. But the things traditionally kept in teachers' desks are those that can and should be used by the whole class. Even very young children can learn to staple safely and put art gum back carefully after use. (If stealing supplies is a problem, all the more reason for students to see what happens when pencils and clips disappear and to experience the hardship of having things run out.) The point here is that the teacher who spends a few days at the beginning of the year really training students to get supplies for themselves in a responsible way is the winner when he or she doesn't have to spend valuable time taping torn papers, finding the gold stars, or fetching supplies for someone else to use.

USE STORAGE BOXES

Dust-proof storage boxes, available from van and storage companies or through the Sears Catalog Department under "Utility Shelving," are a good buy for teachers. Items that are seldom used, such as once-a-year science equipment, can be stored on top of cupboards. If the boxes are uniform and of a neutral color, they won't make the room seem cluttered or overcrowded. Although they may be somewhat hard to get at stored up high, they are readily available if a sturdy table to stand on is handy or if the custodian is around to help. Stick to the academic-subject area scheme and put science and math boxes up over the science and math cupboards, and so forth. These boxes are also time savers in a bungalow or open space room with few cupboards. They are better made and thus more durable than regular storage boxes. The covers are hinged at the back, so the boxes can be opened with one hand.

USE CONTAINERS FOR ODD THINGS

In every classroom there are miscellaneous things floating around. Take a critical look and devise a storage plan for such odd things. For example, on rainy days, place near the door a plastic wastepaper basket for wet umbrellas. Line a large cardboard box with plastic or foil and use if for wet, muddy shoes and rubbers. Baskets of any size will hold whatever doesn't fit somewhere else. Coffee cans make good containers for pencils, paint brushes, crayons, or scissors. Ice-cream cartons can be used to hold books, papers, or magazines. Turned on side, they become "children's cubbies."

MANAGING
THE CLASSROOM

When teachers hear *classroom management*, they often think *discipline*. The usual meaning of *to manage* is to conduct or direct the affairs of something or someone. To us, classroom management really means to carry on the business of teaching in the most efficient way. This chapter identifies the various tasks classroom teachers manage yet needn't necessarily do themselves, and it suggests ways to use helpers in performing these tasks. (Discipline is the subject of Chapter 7, page 87).

THE TEACHER'S ROLE

The role of the teacher has changed drastically in the last 10 years, and our old vision of what a teacher should be and do no longer holds. One reason people choose a particular profession is the image they entertain of themselves practicing that profession. Many teachers, for example, see themselves as the patient school parent kindly fulfilling all the needs of all their students. Others teachers picture themselves as understanding mentors, solving all the personal as well as academic problems of their students. Still others view themselves as stewards of the intellect, who not only impart knowledge but also fire their students with an enthusiasm for learning. These and other images of the teaching profession are not merely fantasies, they are mental models, ideals to be lived up to.

It is terribly hard to make compromises with ideals, just as it is terribly hard to give up some of the things for which one became a teacher in the first place. But since the reassuring straightforwardness and the appealing simplicity of these views just don't jibe with the realities of the modern classroom, they can become a major source of anxiety for teachers who can't live up to them and a major impediment to functioning successfully as today's teachers.

The role of the teacher as a "learning manager" is a new role—one more realistic, more congruent with the multiplicity of demands a teacher faces today. In this revised image the teacher is at the top of an organizational ladder, in the number-one position of a small business. (Always keep in mind, of course, that student learning is the purpose of the business.) Just beneath the teacher are those people who are immediately available for assuming some of the burden of running the classroom: the students in that classroom, their parents, other students within the school, volunteers and other teachers. One step below them are the school site support people such as principals, counselors, nurses, and librarians. Last come district level support people such as curriculum consultants, research department staff, audio-visual and textbook clerks, and materials workshop people. A chart of this kind of organization might look like this:

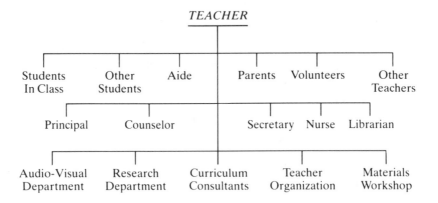

TEACHER

Students In Class	Other Students	Aide	Parents	Volunteers	Other Teachers
	Principal	Counselor		Secretary	Nurse	Librarian
Audio-Visual Department	Research Department	Curriculum Consultants	Teacher Organization	Materials Workshop

If a teacher becomes, at least in his or her own mind, a mini-administrator, using the people available, consciously delegating work wherever possible, and streamlining the planning and paper-work, then all sorts of changes for the better are possible.

NONTEACHING TASKS

A good place to start using helpers is with the nonteaching tasks that make up a teacher's day. (Some estimates say these jobs comprise 35 percent of a teacher's workload.) Begin as the school day starts and list, as they occur, all the things that you do that do not require professional expertise. Your list may be similar to this one:

- ☐ open windows and adjust blinds
- ☐ write calendar and assignments on the chalkboard
- ☐ make and run dittos
- ☐ put out materials, equipment, and supplies
- ☐ mix paints
- ☐ supervise coatroom; help with coats and boots
- ☐ put paper on easels
- ☐ conduct opening exercises
- ☐ collect money
- ☐ play a word game
- ☐ write a story as a child dictates
- ☐ watch as a child traces a word to make sure the letters are formed correctly
- ☐ interview a child and help choose a book of interest
- ☐ explain a manipulative math activity to a child
- ☐ supervise the playground during recess
- ☐ put notices for home in student mailboxes
- ☐ frame a finished picture
- ☐ supervise clean-up of paints and brushes
- ☐ write a note for a sick child to give to the nurse
- ☐ fill out a checklist for the office
- ☐ listen to a child practice pronunciation
- ☐ pass out lunch tickets; check lunch money

- ☐ help hunt for a child's lost lunch
- ☐ read a story to a group
- ☐ help children who are reading
- ☐ rearrange the table for group committee work
- ☐ supervise a working committee meeting of children preparing a puppet show
- ☐ pass out papers to go home
- ☐ pull papers, explain seatwork, and mark pages in books for a child who is going on a trip and will need homework

While your job list will vary according to grade level and assignment, making such a list forces you to analyze what you do and makes you think about distributing as many of these tasks as you can among the people available to help you.

All this is not to say that the remaining 65 percent of a teacher's job is pure teaching nor that a credential is essential to the success of all remaining teaching-related tasks. For example, it doesn't take a professional to do much of the drill work on words, phrases, or math combinations. There are many teaching-related duties that can be performed by others under the direction of a good managing teacher. Making decisions about what each student needs and about the best way to present the lessons to him or her, however, are judgments that only a teacher can make. In addition, there are many other things happening in a classroom that require a teacher's knowledge. It is a sensible teacher who takes the time to differentiate among the different parts of the job—nonteaching, teaching-related, and pure teaching—and who uses the information to delegate anything that can be delegated to the appropriate helpers.

PARENTS AND COMMUNITY VOLUNTEERS

Frequently teachers say that they feel uncomfortable asking parents and others to help them with their jobs. But look at it another way—volunteers aren't helping you with your job, they are helping students. In recruiting volunteers, explain that you can, by yourself, teach the class as a whole and give students the essentials. But in order to give your students the richest year possible and meet their individual needs the way they should be met, you need help. The workload is too much for one person, but with volunteers to help, together you can all accomplish the impossible. Don't apologize. Using volunteers benefits everyone concerned.

THINGS VOLUNTEERS CAN DO FOR A TEACHER

Clerical Duties

- ☐ order and return books and audio-visual materials
- ☐ make instructional materials
- ☐ keep records of children's work and progress
- ☐ keep records of volunteer time
- ☐ file materials
- ☐ take roll
- ☐ grade papers or tests
- ☐ put information and lessons on chalkboard

Housekeeping Duties

- ☐ clean and dust
- ☐ wash paint jars and brushes
- ☐ straighten closet and cupboards
- ☐ count, sort, and store games and activities
- ☐ decorate room bulletin boards
- ☐ check playground equipment

Supervisory Duties

- ☐ sit with children at a play or assembly
- ☐ watch children at recess
- ☐ attend a field trip and care for a small group
- ☐ eat lunch with a group on rainy days
- ☐ help children learn to clean the room and maintain order

In addition to the routine duties a volunteer can do for a teacher, there are many teaching-related tasks he or she can perform.

Teaching Reinforcement

- ☐ dictate spelling words
- ☐ listen to reading practice
- ☐ give drills on words, phrases, and math flash cards

- ☐ supervise games and small group activities
- ☐ listen to children
- ☐ help with art and music
- ☐ help with written compositions
- ☐ help children who were absent from class to catch up
- ☐ give reinforcement to children new to the class
- ☐ supervise individual testing
- ☐ set up learning centers
- ☐ help children publish a class newspaper
- ☐ supervise student committees doing social studies research
- ☐ work with projectors, recorders, or listening posts
- ☐ repeat a lesson for a child who needs extra help

Tutorial Tasks

- ☐ give one-to-one help in math, reading, and science as a follow-up to concepts already introduced by the teacher
- ☐ build a child's confidence through a relationship of mutual respect
- ☐ give individual help with writing and spelling

Enrichment Tasks

- ☐ share a special skill (sewing, cooking), experience (trip, job), talent (music, art), or information (science, job) through demonstrations, pictures, films, objects, dances, plays, or costumes
- ☐ use a special skill to help children produce a project (for example, write a book of poetry or build an experimental playground toy of vinyl and foam)
- ☐ go to a workshop that the teacher is not able to attend and bring the information back for the class
- ☐ serve as interpreter for bilingual children or teach a second language
- ☐ record foreign language stories
- ☐ be the class expert for the study of a special culture or country (collect materials, prepare food or costumes)
- ☐ accompany class or small groups on a study trip pertaining to a specialty

✂ *SHORTCUTS*

RECRUIT ACTIVELY

Think big. Everyone who has a little extra time is a potential volunteer waiting to be recruited. If you already have a volunteer, let him or her do your recruiting for you. Personal phone calls are more effective than letters or notices. Personal visits are the most effective way to recruit help. Begin with the parents of students in your class and contact them all at the start of the school year, either by phone or at orientation meetings. At the close of the meeting ask parents to write their names and times available on the chalkboard or on a sign-up sheet. If both of a child's parents work, don't give up. Seek out a grandparent, an aunt, and out-of-work relative, or even neighbors and friends of the family. When looking for volunteers, don't forget retired people, senior citizens, and your own friends and neighbors.

TRAIN THEM WELL

Well-trained volunteers can relieve a teacher of virtually all non-teaching tasks, so take a little time at the beginning to train them. Train one or two volunteers very carefully, and then let them train others as they are recruited. Even with such help, be aware that you will have to do some of the training. It is our experience, supported by other teachers, that five is the magic number when it comes to volunteers. With volunteers, the teacher has a nucleus of trained, experienced people to undertake recruiting and training duties, and the program begins to run itself.

Give your volunteers easy tasks—listening to students read or dictating spelling words—until you learn what else they are capable of doing and until they feel very comfortable with you and the children. Follow three simple rules and you will find that not only can you obtain the help of volunteers but that you can keep them coming week after week.

- ☐ Be warm, friendly, and supportive (build confidence).
- ☐ Give each of your volunteers a variety of tasks (keep the job interesting).
- ☐ Show thanks and appreciation with sincere praise often (make volunteering rewarding).

ASK THEM TO WORK
OUTSIDE THE ROOM

Some teachers are reluctant to use volunteers because they do not feel comfortable with other adults in their classrooms. There are many reasons for these feelings, both real and imagined. Such feelings are important and must be reckoned with, but don't let them prevent your using volunteers. Use them anyway, only give them assignments outside the classroom. Clerical duties, small group activities, tutoring, and so forth can all be accomplished just as well in the hall, in a corner of the library, in an unused office, or even outside on the lawn. If you'd rather no one knew you were sensitive to the presence of parental eyes and ears, explain that a quiet corner makes for better concentration. Until using volunteers effectively becomes automatic, refer to the checklist on pages 20-21 for other ways in which to put volunteers to work most efficiently.

HAVE THEM HELP AT HOME

If parents and other volunteers can't come to you, give them a chance to help at home. While this may seem like a second-best way to obtain help, teachers with several of these back-up volunteers agree that they carry a large workload and provide important services. Use them for such tasks as making educational materials, mending and repairing instructional games and puzzles, filing and sorting, binding books, mending or washing paintshirts, darning a parachute, looking up recipes for a classroom cooking center and trying them out, phoning other parents, doing research at the library for a class unit, or baby-sitting for a parent who is volunteering for you at school.

PAVE THE WAY FOR THEM

Prepare your class for volunteers by saying something like, "Mrs. Jones could be working for herself at home or doing other things she likes to do this morning, but she came to school to help us instead because she cares about you. She is not here to teach you how to behave. I have already done that. So, if you do not help her by doing your best, I have asked her to remove you from the group and you will have to make up the lesson on your own time." This kind of introduction gives volunteers some clout with the class yet does not put them in the role of disciplinarian.

KID POWER

Using students to help run the classroom isn't a new idea, but it is an idea that deserves more than casual or sporadic attention. If you give plenty of thought to all the ways you might enlist and use student help, develop a plan, and put the plan into effect, you'll find that judicious use of student helpers will save you all sorts of work.

✂ *SHORTCUTS*

ASSIGN PERMANENT JOBS TO STUDENTS

Give over the jobs of tying shoes, sharpening pencils, putting on bandages, opening windows, adjusting blinds, checking desks, and scrubbing sinks to the children. To keep student help from being more trouble than it's worth, give each student a *permanent* job for the year. Spend parts of the first days of school assigning a job to every student, then take the necessary time to train each one carefully to handle the assigned job exactly as you want it done. Even very young students can be trained to be perfectionists if they're convinced their jobs are important. Keep a record of job assignments in your plan book. Use one set of names and corresponding jobs for the whole year. This record makes assignments easy to remember, and a quiet reminder to a lax student takes little effort and no class time. You'll find that you'll be glad not to have to change a duty wheel or schedule every week. You won't miss having to keep track of who should have done what. Unproductive discussions about who has been negligent in performing a job can be forgotten.

SUGGESTED PERMANENT JOB LIST

Primary Classroom

- ☐ messenger: carry messages to and from office, other classes; pick up mail and movies
- ☐ calendar keeper: follow opening routine with day of week, and so forth; enter date on bulletin board if necessary
- ☐ flag keeper: lead pledge, take care of flag
- ☐ window monitor: open in morning, adjust during day for noise level and weather, close before leaving
- ☐ sink monitor: check for cleanliness every day after class

- ☐ chair monitor: take down in morning, push under table during day, match chairs to correct tables, put up on desks before leaving (has helper)
- ☐ desk monitor: check for neatness inside and out, give award or note for neatness after surprise check (weekly)
- ☐ book monitor: straighten and maintain order
- ☐ movie monitor: return movies to mailbox in office or to other teachers
- ☐ keeper of audio-visual materials: assist teacher with setting up and storage
- ☐ plant tender: feed and water, place in sun
- ☐ roll monitor: take attendance for row or table
- ☐ nurse: teacher checks wound first; monitor to clean and put on bandaid if teacher orders one
- ☐ keeper of lights and doors: turn on and off, open and close, checks during fire drill to make sure door is closed
- ☐ coatroom monitor: check for neatness, watch during going and coming to ensure good citizenship
- ☐ mail clerk: take bulletins from designated place and distribute in mailboxes daily
- ☐ cleaners: several monitors, each responsible for one drawer (crayons, bean sticks, teacher's desk drawers)
- ☐ paper and supplies keeper: replenish supplies, go with teacher to supply room to help carry if school rules prohibit students to do this alone, keep supplies and papers neat, supervise distribution of paper, check to be sure there is no waste
- ☐ ball monitors: take ball out, see that anyone who wants to play has an opportunity to play, carry ball back to class at end of recess (one monitor for each ball)
- ☐ playground equipment keeper: keep ball box neat; distribute jump ropes, bean bags, parachute to students who wish to use them; make sure they are returned
- ☐ pencil sharpener: sharpen pencils—trained to use electric sharpener carefully (a wise investment); if manual sharpener is used, have two monitors (tiring)
- ☐ chalkboard monitor: erase board at end of day, replace erasers and chalk

- [ ] wastebasket monitor: combine waste in one or two baskets if possible and place in hall for caretaker
- [ ] listening post monitor: check earphones and recorders; set up daily with tapes teachers desires; return cassettes, read-a-longs, and so forth to library or office; responsible for keeping tapes organized
- [ ] art custodian: cover tables as needed, help put out supplies, check after cleanup
- [ ] science custodian: take out, clean, store science equipment; care for animals or displays (with a committee)
- [ ] game monitor: keep game shelf neat, mend games, check for lost pieces
- [ ] substitutes: usually two to fill in when monitors are absent

Intermediate Classroom

For intermediate classes, add these tasks to those suggested for primary classes.

- [ ] intercom clerk: answer phone and relay messages
- [ ] catcher-up: explain assignments and help students who missed class for special activities (nurse, glee club, counselor) or who were absent; you need a substitute for this job and may need more than one regular monitor
- [ ] lunch ticket clerk: distribute tickets, remind borrowers to return money
- [ ] artist's helper: prepare materials as needed from teacher's description
- [ ] set-up person: put out materials and equipment as asked for a particular center; you might need a monitor for each center
- [ ] class friend: orient new students, explain routines, gather needed books, be new student's special friend for first few days
- [ ] paint keeper: mix tempera, clean watercolor pans, wash brushes
- [ ] audio-visual projectionist: run projectors with supervision
- [ ] librarian: check books out of and into classroom, remind those who have books overdue at school library

MAKE ALL STUDENT JOBS IMPORTANT

Occasionally teachers are reluctant to make classroom jobs permanent and give up the old duty wheel. They feel that some jobs have more importance and desirability in the minds of children than others and that these more attractive jobs should be traded around during the year. This problem can be handled by upgrading the less desirable jobs and downgrading the more popular ones. For example, more students might prefer to be ball monitor than coatroom monitor. Upgrade the coatroom job by adding to the primary job checking and straightening coats and boots; let that monitor also be on duty when students hang up their coats, get their lunches, and prepare to leave. Coatroom monitoring thus becomes an important job. On the other hand, the ball monitor need not automatically become kickball captain for the entire year—instead he or she is merely charged with the duty of carrying the ball out and back, and putting it away. The teacher will have established impartial rules concerning what is to be played with the ball and who is to play. See pages 25-26 for a sample list of possible permanent jobs for primary and intermediate classrooms.

HAVE TEACHING RECESSES

You will not need to teach what students can teach each other—definitely a Shortcut. Have a "teaching recess" one or two times a week for pairs of students within the class. Team a few teaching students with a few learning students. Assign such tasks as tying shoes, skipping, fitness tests, ball skills, or four-square rules. Don't provide detailed descriptions of what is to be taught and how it is to be done. Let the kids do it their way. A simple statement, made quietly to the students involved, such as "Please help Susan with her kicking at 10:00 A.M. today," will suffice. Change the role of learner to teacher occasionally. It's very important to be sure that the "teachers" are patient and sensitive to the feelings of the learners.

MAKE HELPFUL PAIRINGS

Placing a disruptive student between two more stble ones for disciplinary reasons is a common practice; trying placing a less able child between two proficient students and see how much can be learned by "osmosis."

The number of non-English speaking students is on the increase. Pairing these students with bilingual students who act as interpreters enables non-English speakers to participate in the class activities. This pairing is especially helpful if the teacher is not bilingual. Watching the bilingual student do written work, the ESL student is gradually integrated into the mainstream and becomes capable of independent work.

"Buddy" reading, in which two students read to one another in turn, provides an audience for the better reader and a chance for the less able reader to learn vocabulary. Learning takes place without the teacher having to actively teach. Buddy math drill and spelling dictation are other possibilities. This method also provides the teacher with a chance to observe student and record information.

INVITE STUDENT HELPERS FROM OTHER CLASSES

Carry the idea of students helping one another even further and have students from other classes help, too. Choose one or two quiet, efficient, capable students from previous years to stop by your classroom each day before and after school. Train them at the beginning of the year to do specific tasks. Having former students stop by to help can be time-consuming and unproductive unless they can work alone and have a prearranged routine that they perform before they move on to their own classes. Have them do such things as open windows; adjust blinds; check papers with an answer key; and set up a learning center, an animal yard, or an activity table. Discourage random drop-ins before and after school. Don't make the mistake of choosing a former student who is a problem in any way or who needs to have special attention.

TAKE ADVANTAGE OF SPLIT DAYS

If you have a split-day arrangement at your school, use the older students who don't begin school until the second hour to help in your room with the early students. Do the same in the afternoon if you have a split hour at the end of the day. During the day, a primary teacher can arrange to use one different upper-grade student each day at a specific time for a specific job. No student should be asked to miss his or her own class activities more than one hour a week. A teacher who misuses or overuses students from other classes can upset other teachers and ruin the program for others, so be thoughtful. Former students are more help because they are accustomed to the routine of your class, are familiar with the ways you teach, and have a good idea of what is expected of the younger students. However, don't let the lack of suitable former students prevent your using older students. Whether they are your former students or not, well-trained older children are invaluable helpers.

PAIR UP TWO CLASSES

Try teaming an upper-grade class with a lower-grade class for one twenty-minute period each week. Pair the children in the two classes and make as few changes as possible during the entire year. The older child develops a sense of responsibility and real concern for his or her younger partner' and the teachers, once the program has been worked out and is running smoothly, will find that they both have a Shortcut to teaching academic skills and to changing attitudes.

MATCH STUDENTS WITH
SIMILAR INTERESTS

If centers are used at a particular time each day, an upper-grade student may be assigned to supervise one or more centers. An older student who has a special hobby or interest can be paired with a child who has the same interest and who finishes his or her work quickly, and the two can use the time to research and develop their mutual interest. The teacher is freed from some of the extra work that such fast finishers require.

START A CROSS-AGE
TUTOR PROGRAM

If there are people available at your school site to organize and run the cross-age tutor programs, use them. Don't hesitate to organize the program yourself, however, because in the long run it will save much more time and energy than it demands.

LET STUDENTS HELP WITH CATCH-UPS

When students miss an assignment because they are out of the room because of such things as glee club, orchestra, examination by the nurse, or illness, let other students help them catch up. Plan a time for this—perhaps the first few minutes in the morning for absentees and the last few minutes of the day for those out of the room for special activities. Responsible and very capable students should be given these jobs permanently so that, once trained, they can supply workbook pages, supplies, and so forth, without help from you. Train these helpers to check work and enter made-up assignments in your records. Appoint back-up substitutes for these students, in case of absences. Don't appoint student helpers until school has been in session long enough for you to know their strengths and weaknesses. This is a Shortcut only if you find just the right people to fit the job.

AIDES

Unlike parents and volunteers who help occasionally in the room, aides are on duty daily. The continuity in their work along with the payment they receive places them in a unique position. They are para-professionals. "Para" in Latin means "beside," and that is how you should consider your aides—they are not clerks or housekeepers; they stand beside you professionally.

✂ SHORTCUTS

TRAIN YOUR AIDE WELL

To be sure, some of your aide's tasks should include clerical and housekeeping duties, but his or her main function should be to reinforce the teaching. Give your aide careful training that includes:

1. A school tour that points out the supply room, book room, cafeteria, and so forth. Introduce your aide to key people.
2. An explanation of your storage system for materials, books, and supplies.
3. An outline of class procedures and routines—time schedules, movement routines, and so forth.
4. A discussion of discipline policies.
5. An explanation of the aide's own daily chores, such as picking up mail, supervising opening exercises, and mixing paints. Have these specific duties written down in a plan book.
6. A discussion of your record-keeping system.

7. An arrangement for the secretary or other office person to teach the aide how to use office machines, such as duplicators, thermofaxes, and laminators.

8. A thorough plan of how you want to be helped with student instruction. You may begin by letting your aide observe you as you teach. Teach your aide a few sample lessons, then let the aide teach them to students. Discuss. Always give the aide a brief written outline of the lesson. Some lessons will be spelled out for the aide in a teacher's guide; show him or her how to use such guides.

MEET DAILY

School districts often provide one aide per teacher for two or three hours a morning. If you are fortunate enough to have an aide, make time in your daily schedule to discuss with the aide the day's lessons and the aide's specific duties. Before class begins is a good time to hold these discussions; or, if a volunteer is available to handle the opening, use the first few minutes of class time. If there's no time before class and no volunteer to take over, let your class wait quietly for a few minutes; you will save more time than these talks require during an efficiently run morning. Put your plan book out, make it available to aides and volunteers, and mark all helpers' duties with different colored pencils in your plan book so they can refer to it without disturbing you. (See Chapter 6, "Planning," page 77.)

ESTABLISH YOUR AIDE'S AUTHORITY

Give your aide the support necessary to perform with you as part of a team by preparing your class to accept him or her as another teacher with all the authority that title implies. If both of you maintain the same standards and exercise the same responsibility, then discipline and academic performance will reflect your consistency. Do not try to be the disciplinarian or overseer for everyone in the room. Set the standards and let everyone work towards them with you. (See Chapter 7, "Discipline," page 87.)

OTHER TEACHERS

Other teachers are always a good source of ideas. They can also be the source of innumerable Shortcuts if you nourish the team spirit and set up a share-and-exchange system. It's all too easy to find yourself isolated in your classroom. Making a determined effort to share work with your colleagues will help you break through that isolation and will help lighten your workload.

✂ SHORTCUTS

SHARE WORK ON CENTERS

If you use centers, meet with a colleague who teaches the same grade and decide what center you will both use. To begin, each of you will develop separate materials and plans for all the centers. At the end of the week, or whatever time span you use, exchange these materials and plans and give yourself a week off from center preparations. Do the same with art projects. If you teach art one day a week, plan with another teacher what you'd like to do for a couple of weeks. You provide materials for both classes one week; your teacher friend does so for the other week.

TRY INTERCLASS GROUPING

When two teachers teach reading at the same time, one or two children can be exchanged to make groupings more compatible. This kind of cooperative grouping can save you one preparation and one teaching job each day. Please note that formal team teaching is not being suggested, but rather an informal cooperative arrangement between two teachers. Teachers helping teachers is an excellent way to cut effort and make the work more pleasant.

SCHOOL SITE SUPPORT PEOPLE

Even small districts receive some form of state or federal funds today. These funds often pay for specialists, facilitators, coordinators, and resource teachers. These positions were created to intensify the education of students, and since their very existence is dependent upon their usefulness to teachers and students, it seems strange that some teachers are reluctant to use the extra help available. It is valuable to pinpoint why some teachers hesitate to turn to a seemingly valuable source of help; some roadblocks need to be cleared away before support personnel can be used effectively.

☐ Teachers sell themselves short and fear that seeking help will be construed as incompetence.

☐ Teachers are uneasy about the judgmental attitude and lack of understanding exhibited by some support people.

☐ Teachers resent the interruptions that specialists and others cause when they remove students from class or enter the classroom to teach a lesson.

☐ Teachers don't always agree with techniques used and information taught by specialists, and yet they are reticent to voice their dissatisfaction. (Perhaps the feeling that a specialist's job is a step above and takes priority over their own contributes to their lack of confidence.)

It is the responsibility of people in the helping positions to make you feel secure enough to reveal, without fear of being judged, the areas in which you need help. But you need to trust in the good intentions of most support people and open up enough to turn the relationship into a team effort. The help you receive for your students is enough of a Shortcut to make this worth the effort. Don't worry about not knowing everything there is to know about curriculum, teaching techniques, and so forth. Give yourself credit for the knowledge that you have, recognize your strengths, and acknowledge your weaknesses. Teaching is mostly caring enough to seek needed information and knowing where to find it.

✂ SHORTCUTS

WORK OUT SCHEDULES

Put first things first. If a specialist needs time with your children, consult your schedule and give the specialist a choice of a few times during the week. Let him or her work out a time schedule to fit yours. Be considerate of the feelings of specialists but be firm in your resolve not to let them interrupt your teaching or cause you to reteach because so many students are out for special activities.

MAKE SPECIFIC REQUESTS

Ask specialists to do specific things with specific students. For example, "I tried to get John to understand borrowing. He still doesn't get it. I'd like you to work on borrowing, subtracting one digit from two digit numbers, please.'' You will save time and get better results if you make your requests as precise as possible.

IDENTIFY WHAT SUPPORT STAFF
CAN DO FOR YOU

Know the duties of the support staff. The word that usually best describes the school secretary is ''swamped,'' yet there are things he or she should be doing for you: sending letters home, typing or dittoing minutes of meetings, answering questions by phone, and ordering special supplies, to name a few. Facilitators can arrange the details for a field trip with your class.

INVITE THE NURSE TO HELP

Ask the school nurse to weigh and measure students at the beginning of the school year. Use the information for math, health, or science lessons throughout the year. The nurse is also a good source of lessons. Ask him or her to give a special lesson on ''Foods for Teeth'' or ''Eat to Stay Thin.'' The nurse will probably be willing to give a follow-up lesson and perhaps even a regular lesson every other month or so.

LET THE LIBRARIAN DO
SOME RESEARCH

The librarian can research special projects for you, given enough prior notice. Let him or her hunt up literature on special topics, such as dragons. It may be possible to pull in books from other libraries within the district. It is faster for the librarian to tell you what new books, filmstrips, or other materials would best fit your need than it is for you to look over lists of new entries and descriptions and try to guess what might fit. Chances are the librarian has already previewed the material.

KEEP IN TOUCH WITH
YOUR PRINCIPAL

Maintain close contact with your principal. Most administrators like to feel helpful; give them the opportunity whenever it will save you time. Principals or their staffs know where things are stored in a building, how to get new supplies from the district, what the district or state framework states for each subject at each grade level, what the legal ramifications of a situation are, and so forth. You can ferret out this information on your own, but using the administrator's knowledge saves you time. You should know the special strengths of you principal and use them. Some are experts in school law; others have a subject matter specialty; others pride themselves in community relations.

It may be difficult to find time to talk with administrators— don't wait in line; use the mailbox. Ask questions in a short note. This approach has the added benefit of giving the principal time to locate information for you from another source if necessary.

Keep your principal informed about what you are doing in your classroom so that any questions can be answered before they become problems. This prevents your having to replan, retrench, and reschedule.

CAPITALIZE ON THEIR EXPERTISE

Use school support personnel for career planning interviews in your class. The librarian, nurse, custodian, secretary, and counselor have valuable career training which they can share with your class. Asking them to give classroom interviews saves you phone time. You would have to locate appropriate people in the community who would be willing to grant interviews, set up a convenient time for them to come to school, and call the day before to remind them to come. When you use on-site people, you can accomplish all this with one walk down the hall.

DISTRICT SUPPORT PEOPLE

District level support staffs are usually somewhat removed from the school. However, they are important to you as a source of information, information that would take you a lot of extra time and effort to find on your own. Call on them for the help they are intended to provide.

✂ SHORTCUTS

GET HELP FROM CURRICULUM CONSULTANTS

Curriculum consultants have the time to do research for you, and they have the facilities to make long-distance calls at district expense. Let them find out the results of an experimental program you saw briefly on television or heard about at a conference. Before you go to the trouble of writing and submitting an application, ask them to check with the budget department to see if there is any money left for attendance at conferences. Request that they locate a copy of a new series of books or materials for you. Seek their opinion about an instructional kit you saw at another school.

USE THE RESEARCH DEPARTMENT

The research department can give you an item analysis of tests your students have taken, thus saving you time spent pinpointing individual student weaknesses and curriculum gaps. Before changing school programs, consult the research department to find if the changes proposed will mean more detailed records and thus increase your workload. Check with researchers when you are contemplating program changes. They may have valuable research data about the effects of similar changes that were tried elsewhere.

MATERIALS

It has been a long time since children went to school and sat on wooden benches, wrote and did sums on slates, and all read from one reader. Materials and supplies were, to say the least, limited in those early schools. In recent years there has been an explosion of educational aids and materials. Textbooks, workbooks, kits for individualizing instruction, manipulative materials, games, films, tapes, filmstrips, teaching machines, and computers fill our classrooms. Providing materials for schools is big business.

Certainly this is progress—why shouldn't advances in technology, research, and business be used to further the education of our young? Good tools can help make learning adventuresome and exciting. Material that normally might be tedious to young learners can become exciting and easier to understand when supplemented with games, hands-on manipulatives, challenging practice sheets, computer programs, and colorful texts. Certainly, no one would advocate going back to primers and slates.

Each new tool, however, has the potential of bringing with it "side effects" that can add to teacher workload and may, in fact, retard student learning. Unless good materials are well managed, they will use up precious time and make slaves of teachers and students.

In spite of claims by educational supply companies and their sales persons, there are few materials that can immediately lighten a teacher's workload. Even the simplest materials require that a teacher read the manufacturer's instructions, think through the learning benefits, establish a plan for their best use, and anticipate difficulties that students will have in using the materials. Unless the teacher thoroughly studies materials before teaching with them, the materials may merely provide empty exercises in "being busy." Even materials that provide practice on a concept already learned require close supervision to ensure that students are practicing correctly. Individualized learning materials still need management in order to be effective. No matter how interesting materials may look in the box or the sales brochure, they are valueless unless they can be put to work successfully in a roomful of learners. Clearly, the quantity and quality of instructional materials a teacher chooses to bring into the classroom will have a direct bearing on the learning that will occur. Good judgment will save time and energy and promote maximum results.

STORAGE AND ORGANIZATION

Too many materials can create storage and organization problems. When the sheer number of materials in a room makes it impossible to find and use those materials easily and efficiently, their purpose is defeated. What cannot be found when needed is useless. What is displayed in the midst of clutter loses its appeal for learners. It is indeed a challenge to arrange a learning environment that contains large numbers of valuable instructional materials and still not sacrifice order, efficiency, and sound learning principles.

Further, the more materials, the more the upkeep. Instructional kits with answer keys, test booklets, colored pencils, and so forth tend to need regular replenishing. Dominoes, dice, and other game pieces get lost. Game boards get torn, bent, folded, spindled, multilated—or they just plain wear out. It goes without saying that poorly maintained equipment produces slipshod results in learning.

✂ SHORTCUTS

CLEAN OUT THE EXCESS

Resolve that anything occupying space in your classroom will be worthy of that space. Look in the backs of cupboards to find those games that were played once and put away for ever because it took too long for students to learn how to play them, and once learned were too quickly finished. Throw them away. Discard the activity that requires 25 little pieces, a half a dozen of which are always missing. Get rid of the game that creates too much noise and disturbs ongoing classroom learning. And above all, dispose of games that fail to teach or reinforce but, are instead just busy work.

As you go through your files, watch for activity instructions that require you to make 15 cards for each of four players. Weed it out! Be discriminating about those conference or workshop handouts. If you don't have a real need for them, don't bring them home to clutter up your files. Don't jump on the "if-it's-new-it's-great" bandwagon.

Go through the box of extra ditto sheets—the ones left over because some children were absent the day they were used. Choose the ones that were winners, mount them on tagboard and laminate or staple them inside an acetate sleeve, and throw out the rest. The sheets you keep, now reusable, can be put into a center or handed out as individual practice sheets.

Put all leftover scraps or paper, string, and precut forms from art projects into an art collage box. Trying to save a partial set of materials for your next year's class will take more time and space than it's worth. If you want to use that art lesson again, it's as easy to prepare enough for the whole class as it is to try to find and count the few left over from a previous lesson.

BE SURE YOU CAN FIND
WHAT YOU HAVE

Having decided to keep some valuable materials, devise some way of reminding yourself what and where they are. Make good use of labels, color codes, and cluster storage (see pages 13-15). Make a note in the teacher's guide or your plan book if you have something that enhances a particular lesson. Tell where it can be found.

CONTROLLING THE INVENTORY

Clearly, the proliferation of materials can be a real problem. One way to save time and effort and avoid confusion is to provide versatile materials—ones that have more than one use. Taking time to consider in advance what materials can give multiple use will save countless hassles later on.

✂ SHORTCUTS

DON'T USE FIVE WHEN
ONE WILL DO

Given the constraints of time and storage space, don't duplicate what you have. If you have found material that gets the point across efficiently and soundly for children, rejoice and stop looking. For example, it isn't necessary to have beans, Unifix cubes, quiet counters, and acorns for children to use as counters for figuring out math combinations. Decide you will use one of those materials, be sure you have enough to meet all possible needs, teach the children how to use them, decide on a place and way to store them (making sure the students know), and then resist the temptation to bring into the room another kind of material for doing the same thing. Spend the time you save perfecting the use of what you have. Remember, there are advantages for students when their teacher knows what they are doing, and repeated use of a good instructional tool tends to increase a teacher's ability to maximize the benefits of that tool for learners. It also frees children from having to learn how to manipulate another kind of material and reduces the possibility that things will be played with rather than learned from. On the other hand, do not close your mind to new and innovative materials. Keep upgrading and adding, but carefully. It is true that children are sometimes more motivated by something new.

MULTIPLY THE USES OF COUNTING CUBES

When deciding what to throw out and what to keep, try to choose materials that are versatile and adaptable to many purposes. Plastic counting cubes, available from any teacher supply store or catalogue, illustrate this versatility. They are excellent to use as counters in math activities, to demonstrate regrouping in addition and borrowing in subtraction, and to make multiplication and division more concrete. In lower primary grades, these cubes can be used for patterning activities, color discrimination, one-to-one correspondence, place value, and simple counting activities. The cubes also can serve as markers for gameboards. Thus, one kind of material serves many needs.

WORK WITH WORD CARDS

Word cards that frequently accompany reading series can, with good organization, be adapted to serve many needs: sight vocabulary practice, vocabulary extension, alphabetizing practice, and lessons in verbs and nouns. Placed in a center, word cards can provide practice in forming sentences.

CONSIDER DRIED BEANS

Budget limited? Dried beans can serve as counters for math. Fastened on tongue depressors, they become place-value manipulatives. With a little glue and paper, beans become a creative art medium.

TRY DOMINOES, DICE, CARDS

Dominoes, dice, and playing cards are multipurpose materials of the highest order. Use them for teaching number recognition, adding or subtracting dots or pips, comparing numbers, finding differences, putting numbers in order—the possibilities are endless.

USE ONE GAME BOARD

There doesn't need to be a different game board for practicing each different skill. Make or buy a classroom set of about 15 of a single kind of gameboard. All instructions on the board itself should be general enough (''Lose one turn,'' ''Move back five spaces,'' and so forth) to apply to many games with different contents. Use that board to practice reading, phonics, social studies, math, health, or whatever needs practice. Put the content of the game on cards that can be easily made and easily stored. Laminate the cards and the boards to increase their life span, and you have a versatile, fun practice activity that serves many purposes. Teach the whole class the general rules that apply to the gameboard early in the year and forever eliminate the query, ''How do you play this game?'' Veterans can teach new students.

PLAY BINGO MANY WAYS

Use the popular game of Bingo to provide practice for many things. Make or buy a set of blank Bingo cards that have been laminated so they can be written on and erased. To make the cards yourself, simply laminate sheets of one-inch graph paper onto cardboard rectangles. Keep the size of the boards relatively small, depending on grade level—three squares by three, four by four, or at most five by five. Forget the boxes across the top where the letters *B-I-N-G-O* are usually found. There's more practice for students if they need to look over the entire board to find an answer than if they are directed to one column.

Save your time by having students make their own Bingo boards. Suppose you want to practice letter recognition in an early primary grade. Instruct each child to print the letter *b* in any blank. Print the letter correctly on the chalkboard for everyone to copy. Check for student accuracy. Have students put a *t* in any other box; continue until they fill all the boxes. What may seem to the children an activity to help their teacher is, in reality, practice in learning letters. When all the boxes are filled, the caller says, "Look for the letter *t*. Cover it with a bean" (or small construction paper square). Or, "Cover the letter that says *nnnn*." The degree of difficulty is increased if the caller says something such as "Listen to the beginning of the word *bicycle*. Cover the letter that is the same as the one that begins *bicycle*." Practice ending sounds in the same way.

To practice adding, subtracting, multiplying, or dividing, guide the students in filling in the squares with the appropriate numbers. The caller says: "Look for the number that equals four plus seven" (or six times three, or nine minus eight, whatever it is you are working on). Visual stimulus can be added by writing the equation on the chalkboard.

To practice place value use cards with various one-, two-, and three-digit numbers written in the squares. The caller says, "Mark the number with a four in the ten's place" (or eight in the hundred's place, and so forth).

Practice word analysis and language skills by putting words from spelling or vocabulary lists on the bingo board. The caller can ask for words with identical beginning sounds, or can state a definition and ask for the word that matches. Practice rhyming words, antonyms, synonyms, and homonyms all in the same way.

Keep the practice sessions relatively short. Before putting the boards away be sure the students clean them with paper towels or tissue.

MAKE VERSATILE PRACTICE WHEELS

Practice wheels for individual drill have been around for a long time. Instead of making a separate wheel for each practice need, make a set of laminated wheels without numbers or letters. As various needs for practice arise, inscribe letters or numbers with grease crayon or pen. Erase the wheels when finished to make them ready for new uses. For self-checking, put the answers on the backs of the wheels.

USE STUDENT-MADE DRILL CARDS

Instead of buying or making the popular cards filled with small holes that have math problems on one side and answers on the other, let the students make their own. They'll be learning as they make the game, and you'll be saving time and money.

Suppose students need practice in multiplying by six. With nothing more than a pencil, a 6 × 6 inch square of construction paper, and 15 minutes of school time, they can make their own cards.

They put the problem on the front, say 6 × 9 = , and poke a hole with the tip of the pencil under the problem where the answer would normally be, then turn the card over and record 54 beside the hole. Students can use the cards to practice on their own at home or at school, or they can use them with partners.

Drill Cards

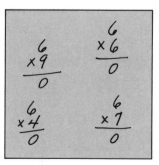
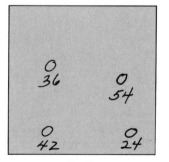

Front   Back

One student puts the point of the pencil in the hole under the number 42 and says to his partner, "What number do I see?" The other player sees the pencil tip at the hole marked 6 × 7 = and must answer, "You see 42."

Besides making math cards, students can make cards for homonyms, synonyms, and definitions, for matching states with capital cities, and so forth.

ADD A NEW TWIST TO
AN OLD ASSIGNMENT

Embellish and extend a good activity to extract full benefit from it. For example, without having to come up with new creative writing assignments all the time, you can assign variations on stories or essays students have already written. Instruct them to rewrite their stories with these changes*:

1. Reverse the sequence of events.
2. Add five new details.
3. Make it funny (or funnier), sad (or sadder).
4. Write it in the form of a telephone conversation.
5. Make it very formal (or informal).
6. Use as few words as you can and still tell your story.
7. Write it in the form of a letter to a particular person. Describe that person's age, interests, and so forth.
8. Write it so that someone reading the story will want to go out and do something (will be moved to action).

FIGURE THE VARIATIONS OF
A SINGLE PROBLEM

Computation practice is a necessary part of a successful math program at all levels. Providing problems for students to use for homework or practice can be time-consuming. Consider making one drill sheet with 10 to 15 problems—number and difficulty will

---

*This idea is adapted from an article by Robert H. Weston, entitled "Creative Writing Revisited," *Learning Magazine,* May/June, 1975.

depend on grade level and student need—and vary the practice by varying the instructions for doing the problems. For example:

1. Add.   463
   + 187

2. Reverse top digits and add.   364
   + 187

3. Reverse bottom digits and add.   463
   + 781

4. Use digits to form largest number and add.   643
   + 871

5. Use digits to form smallest number and add.   346
   + 178

6. Double the first number and add.   926 (463 doubled)
   + 187

7 .Double the bottom number and add.
                                         463
   + 374 (187 doubled)

8. Double both numbers and add.   926
   + 374

9. Subtract as is, if possible. If bottom number   463
   is larger than top number, reverse numbers.   − 187

10. Reverse digits and subtract.   364
    Reverse numbers if necessary.   − 781

11. Double the top number and subtract.   926
    − 187

12. Double the bottom number and subtract.   463
    − 374

13. Multiply by digit in one's column only.   463
    ×   7

14. Multiply by digit in ten's column only.   463
                                                 $\times$ 80

15. Multiply by digits in one's and ten's column.   463
                                                       $\times$ 87

16. Multiply by all digits.   463
                               $\times$ 187

17. Divide top number by each of bottom digits.
                               7 $\overline{)\,463}$ 8 $\overline{)\,463}$ 1 $\overline{)\,463}$

18. Divide by digit in ten's column only.   80 $\overline{)\,463}$

19. Divide by digit in hundred's column only.   100 $\overline{)\,463}$

20. Divide top number by bottom number.   187 $\overline{)\,463}$

21. Write as a fraction and simplify. $\dfrac{463}{187}$

You can put the list of instructions on a large chart for easy reference when making assignments — "Do the problems on your drill sheet according to instruction number 6." To vary the practice, an assignment might require students to do one problem, which you have written on the chalkboard, in each of the ways explained on the instruction sheet.

ROLL OUT THE PAPER

Shorten the time it takes to provide paper each day for each student's drill practice by furnishing each student with a small roll of adding machine tape secured with a rubber band or paper clip. The length of the paper in each roll shouldn't be more than about four feet. Have students leave about an inch between each problem they write. These rolls ought to last several days and save plenty of handing-out time. When filled with problems, strips can be fastened together to try to make a "Mile of Math" (or better still, a "Kilometer of Math").

MAINTENANCE

Maintenance of materials is an ongoing concern. Someone must watch for deterioration and excessive wear, and someone must replenish and repair. That someone needn't always be you. Students, teacher aides, and volunteers can do the job just as easily.

✂️*SHORTCUTS*

MAKE IT LAST

With use, paper will tear, games will get dirty, beans will fall off beansticks, and parts will need to be replaced. Delegate someone to help you maintain your materials. This can be one of the permanent job assignments for a child in your room. Don't let materials deteriorate too far before mending. Encourage students to watch for beginning signs of deterioration. Let them share the responsibility of keeping up the classroom.

If you need many things done, organize a repair workshop and get parent volunteers to spruce up materials. In a short time several parents can do what would take you many hours to accomplish alone.

ENLIST THE TROOPS

Your whole class can be trained to help maintain supplies. On the supply cabinet, pin a paper headed "Supplies We Need." When anyone in the room detects a shortage developing—paper, clips, rubber bands, parts of an individualized study kit, and so forth—instruct that person to make a note on the "Supplies We Need" slip. The student designated to maintain supply levels will thereby have a reminder. There can be a similar system for reporting needed repairs.

MANAGING THE DAILY FLOW

One of the daily tasks of a teacher is having instructional materials ready when they are needed. If not carefully planned, this task can consume great amounts of a teacher's time and effort. A good materials storage plan and a carefuly organized system for sharing the tasks, coupled with strong teacher leadership in directing how things shall be used and put away, provide the necessary foundation for successful preparation of materials. Beyond that there are specific Shortcuts.

✂ SHORTCUTS

DON'T LET DITTOS
ENSLAVE YOU

It is of paramount importance that you control the number of dittos you make. There are many good assignments that can be quickly written on the chalkboard, given orally, or put on tagboard and laminated. Keep enlarging your collection of this kind of lesson. It's very possible that the invention and proliferation of duplicator machines has helped make students too dependent upon someone else to do most of their work and thinking for them. Filling in a blank or making a choice of *a, b,* or *c* does not require the same degree of initiative and thinking as does creating an answer from scratch. Even copying problems from a book or chalkboard, if not overdone, may not be the waste of time some consider it to be. That process may be helping to build responsibility, precision, and carefulness.

Use your workbooks. If they're not consumable, put them in plastic sleeves and correct them as the students are working, either by spot-checking yourself or by having students exchange work in small groups. Use the questions at the ends of chapters. Put open-ended suggestions on tagboard such as:

1. Write another ending for the story.
2. Explain how different weather would have changed the story.

HAVE A PLAN FOR
MAKING AND USING DITTOS

Well-prepared duplicatable practice sheets do have a place in a good instructional program. Make these dittos with a good lead pencil so that a thermofax picture can be made of the sheet if and when the ditto carbon wears out. Some teachers paperclip a sheet of white paper over the ditto master and use a number two pencil to make their original on this sheet; they find it easier to file one thin copy of a pencilled sheet than a messy ditto master. When a new ditto is needed, they simply thermofax the pencilled original. While it is true that regular ditto masters can be saved for a reasonable length of time, the very thin thermofax ditto masters are hardly worth the space and effort it takes to preserve them. Chances are they will not produce a good enough second set of copies to warrant the time and space it took to store them. We suggest that you throw them away after use. You still have your pencilled copy for next time.

Try to plan ahead enough so that one trip by you or your aide to the duplicator work room will be all that is necessary for at least a week. Running in every morning before school for one or two sets of papers is not a good use of your time. Develop a plan for storing these made-ahead dittoed lessons so you can put your hands on them when needed.

TRAIN HELPERS TO MAKE DITTOS

Take whatever time is necessary to see that your aide or volunteer is trained to make ditto copies exactly as you want them made. Show him or her how to run one page and examine it carefully for placement on the page: Is everything showing? Is there room enough all around for answers? Can it be read easily? Impress upon your helpers that if copies become too faint, they should stop immediately and either make a new ditto master or check with you before proceeding. Also, there is no value in making 40 copies when only 36 are needed. Stress this point. If someone on the office staff will do this training for you, fine—just make sure the training is done well.

CONQUER THE PENCIL AND CRAYON PROBLEM

Keeping students supplied with a full supply of colored crayons and pencils sharp enough to write is a challenge in the best of circumstances. Different plans may work with different classes, and it is the wise teacher who continues to work with a class until a reasonably satisfactory system is developed and used by everyone. Experiment with the suggestions below until you hit upon a workable system.

Encourage the class to think of school-furnished crayons and pencils as the property of everyone in the room rather than the personal property of individuals—even though each will have his or her own supply. If this idea is talked about, along with the notion that it's to everyone's advantage to take good care of the classroom working tools, there may be less hoarding, stealing, carelessness, or other problems.

Keep extra crayons left over from previous years in empty half-pint milk cartons. Separate them by color and put them in a box or drawer that everyone can get to. This system saves student time and class disruption if students cannot find one of the needed colors in their own boxes.

Have two containers for pencils, one for sharpened pencils and the other for dull or broken ones. When a supply of new pencils arrives from the office, collect all the old ones for the containers. Tell students that the "ticket" for a sharpened pencil is an unsharpened one. Have them put the dull pencils in the appropriate container and take sharpened ones from the other container. Make it clear that pencils will only be sharpened by the pencil monitor or the teacher. To encourage greater care in the person who habitually cannot find a pencil for the exchange or in some way abuses the system, make him or her use a crayon for the rest of the day. Hoarders of pencils will be uncovered during the regular, unannounced desk check that is someone's permanent job (see page 25). If pencils disappear and you suspect some students are taking them home, you may need to have a "pencil check" at the door as the children leave at day's end.

STREAMLINE PREPARATION AND CLEAN-UP OF ART MATERIALS

Even with prolific painters in your room, you should not have to mix paints more than once every 10 days. Use sturdy containers such as half-pint milk cartons or plastic or styrofoam drinking cups for holding the paint. Avoid metal cans, since they have sharp edges that cut and tend to rust around the tops. Fill the cups three-quarters full with paint mixture. Before leaving at night, a monitor shuld fill each paint cup almost to the brim with water to keep the paint from drying out and to dissolve encrusted paint. Some teachers find that adding a drop or two of glycerine to paint tends to make it last longer and maintain a pleasant smell. The monitor should pour off the excess water each morning, leaving only the thick paint at the bottom.

Save clean-up time by covering paint easels with butcher paper or newspaper. Drape a single sheet over the top and sides. Make it long enough to cover the holes that hold the paint cans—it isn't hard to push the paint cans into place through the paper. When the covering becomes too messy (about once a month), discard it and cover again. You'll find this easier than wiping up oilcloth or even cleaning easels covered with contact paper. Appoint a student easel monitor to maintain easels.

CHOOSE ART PROJECTS CAREFULLY

There can be no quarrel with the notion that art deserves an important place in the curriculum. Preparation for art projects, however, does not deserve an inordinate amount of teachers' planning time. Begin by choosing for children projects that are open-ended, give maximum opportunities for chilen to be creative, and do not require you to do a lot of precutting, pretracing, or premixing.

Don't confuse art lessons with lessons that are primarily exercises in following directions. The objective of a school art class is not to produce 30 cute May baskets for halls or classroom bulletin boards, but rather to provide opportunites for students to engage in a process of making something that will:

1. promote thinking, observing, and seeing
2. enhance self image and promote the idea that each individual is different
3. add to the beauty of this world
4. foster responsibility for cleaning up after oneself

These objectives are best met with moderately simple art projects that call for a variety of media. Collect art ideas from district consultants, teacher magazines, books, colleagues, museums, art galleries, colleges and universities, and, of course, your own imagination. Make sure that you have a good idea of the total process the project involves, not simply a mental image of the final product.

When you try an art project and find that it is successful, take time to preserve the idea. Paste a copy of one of the finished products on the front of a manila folder. Insider the folder write the step-by-step directions, then file it by season or month. The project is now available to put in a center or to give to a volunteer to use with a group of children. Of course, the folder also serves as your guide when you want to repeat the experience with another group of children.

MAKE AUTHORS OF THEM ALL

Most children love to write, draw, or figure in "books" of their own. Homemade booklets with construction paper covers and a few pages of blank writing paper are easy to construct. The only tool you need is a stapler. Get others to help you make them. A group of volunteers, students, your neighbors, or even your own family can make enough booklets in an hour or so to provide you with almost a year's supply. Forget the once popular "shape" booklets unless you have lots of help or unlimited extra personal time. The motivation that is provided by a booklet cut into the shape of a pumpkin, for example, can be provided by talking about pumpkins and then letting students make their own pumpkin pictures on the covers.

The booklets serve well for original stories, math extension, social studies projects, journals, field trip notes, recipes, personal interest research projects, and so forth. Worked into a well-thought-out system for their use, these booklets can save the time it takes to pass out individual papers and provide answers to the often-asked question, "I'm finished. What do I do now, teacher?" The back covers also make a convenient place to keep records of teacher-student conferences.

AUDIO VISUAL MATERIALS AND BOOKS

✂ SHORTCUTS

SHARE THE PAPERWORK

If you are fortunate enough to work in a district that has an audio-visual department, you will undoubtedly want to enrich your instructional program by ordering and showing pertinent films or filmstrips throughout the year. Your science, health, social studies, math, literature, and human relations instruction can all benefit from timely audio-visual materials. Some audio-visual materials "belong to" your classroom, and you'll keep them on hand. Others you must request for specific dates by filling out order forms. If you know that the other teachers of your grade level will want to use some of the same films or filmstrips, share the burden of filling out order forms. If you expect to be teaching the same grade or subject in subsequent years, save the order forms of the ones you liked so they can be easily recopied and reordered. Also, save any notes you make about materials so you won't need to preview them for another year's showing.

COLOR-CODE BOOKS

Keeping the supply of books flowing smoothly in and out of your room can be simplified by placing small colored dots inside the front cover of books. The dots show where the book came from: school bookroom books, red dot; books from out of building, green dot; teacher-owned books, blue dot; books kept permanently in your room, orange dot; and so forth. Using the dot as a guide, children can help, for example, to place all the books with green dots in a pile for sending to the central textbook office. Everyone can be your helper in finding these books. The only time you will have to check titles against a list is when the count doesn't match. Keep a record of your book color code in your plan book for easy reference.

BE READY FOR
THE INVENTORIES

Accept the fact that sometime during the course of the teaching year someone will want to know what teaching guides are in your room, what audio-visual equipment you have, and perhaps how many of what kind of books are in your care. Requests for inventories invariably come at inopportune times. Be ready by keeping similar materials together whenever possible and by consistently returning things to their proper storage places after use.

Choose and label a shelf in one of your cupboards for your teachers' guides. Arrange your guides in exactly the same order as they appear on the inventory list. If *Teaching Values* is first on the list, make it first on your shelf; follow it with the second title on the list, and so forth. Using this sytem, you'll find it much easier to complete a teachers' guide inventory. When you remove one of the guides from its place, mark the place with a piece of paper so that when you're finished with the guide, you can replace it in its proper position.

Designate one cupboard or a shelf of one cupboard for as many of the audio-visual materials as you can. It makes the count much easier if the materials are centralized.

PAPERWORK

It's easy to understand why most of the paper mills of the world are on a seven-day work week. They are busily manufacturing the paper that teachers will use to fulfill their daily job requirements. It may not be much of an exaggeration to say that paperwork in the teaching profession has increased a thousandfold in recent years.

Besides all the record-keeping paperwork teachers must do (covered in Chapter 5, p. 63), there's a veritable mountain of paper teachers must conquer daily. If they don't, that mountain soon becomes a mountain range. Parents want to be informed in writing. Administrators require written answers to written memos. District offices send questionnaires that must be returned yesterday. Teacher organizations keep in close communication with bulletins and newsletters. Classroom papers have to be checked. And on and on and on.

The time it takes to meet the demands of paperwork causes teachers to wonder, ''When will there be time to teach?'' Clearly, paperwork is a problem that is not going to go away in the fore-seeable future, and, therefore, you must deal with paperwork by using all the ingenuity and creative thinking you can muster.

CORRESPONDENCE

The office mailbox is a major source of papers. Here appear at one time or another all the written communications from administrators, other teachers, parents, sales representatives, publishers, professional organizations, and sometimes even a love note from a student. Typically the teacher or aide picks up these papers daily, carries them to the teacher's lounge, forgets them until next recess, and finally brings them to the classroom. Here, if they aren't marooned on the shelf with the first aid kit where they were dropped temporarily while the teacher fixed Johnny's skinned knee, they will be added to the pile of the previous three day's mail. It isn't until a reminder from the school secretary forces some action that the pile is touched, and then it is simply shuffled until the necessary document is found. Eventually, when the pile gets too high to see over, the teacher takes the time to see what's in there. By then, much of the mail is obsolete—the Good Reading in-service is past; the P.T.A. meeting took place the previous night.

Yet some teachers have their reports in on time, never miss a meeting, can put their hands on the principal's bulletin of two months ago, and still keep reasonable hours with calmness and serenity. The secret of their success is organization, otherwise known as having a plan and using it. Nowhere in the teaching scheme is this more important than in dealing with miscellaneous paperwork.

✂ SHORTCUTS

ESTABLISH AN "OFFICE"

Set aside a specific place in the classroom for reading mail and doing paperwork. Your desk seems a logical place for this personal office. However, any place that is near a file cabinet, a wastebasket, and a flat surface for writing will serve nicely. Keep on hand a few office supplies, such as paper, pens, pencils, carbon paper, paper clips, file folders, and envelopes. If you need to sign your name often, consider buying a rubber stamp that prints your name. Any office supply store can make up a stamp, or perhaps your school district will furnish one for you if you ask. Also but a date stamp with an ink pad. A desk organizer is very helpful, too. Mark the slots "To File" and "To Do." The location and appearance of the office is of little importance. What is important is that you think of it as a place where all things having to do with your miscellaneous paperwork are centralized. It makes sense to place in the same spot paperwork that needs action and the materials with which to act. Gone should be the frantic searches for school papers in your car, brief case, or desk at home. No longer should you have to send your aide to the workroom or lounge to see if you inadvertently left the mail there.

SORT MAIL ON THE SPOT

If there is a flat surface in the school office near the mailboxes and you have an extra minute or two, spread out the papers in the mailbox and examine them quickly to find any paper that can be dealt with on the spot. "How many pencils do you need? Answer: 32." Hand the paper to the secretary. "Do you have a teacher's guide to *Tapestry?* Answer: no." Put your reply in the reading specialist's mailbox. You find a thank-you note from Johnny's mother. Stash it in wastebasket after you read it. Already your pile of mail is somewhat reduced. You've saved a trip to your office and back for two pieces, and you are well on your way to being considered one of the prompt ones.

SCHEDULE A MAIL TIME

Since looking at the mail and doing something about it are two different things, this look-through should be a sorting time. There are three things that can be done with a piece of mail in this sorting process. It can be thrown away, saved for future reference, or put in the "To Do" file pending further action. With a little practice you will need only a few minutes to complete most sorting jobs. It's the kind of thing that can be done while children are resting after lunch or during the first 10 minutes of a 20-minute silent reading time. Do sorting regularly and consistently, preferably at approximately the same time each day. Make this a habit.

DON'T JUST SHUFFLE–DECIDE

This is not as easy as it sounds for some teachers, especially when they are forced to decide between throwing something away and saving it for future use. Remember, classes change, children change, and materials change. Saving something that "might come in handy" is a trap that clutters storage systems so the useful things get lost. Make good use of the wastebasket.

Two file folders or two shelves of a desk organizer clearly labeled "To Do" and "To File" are all you need to complete the sorting job. Notice, there's no folder for "Miscellaneous" or "To Be Decided Later." Whoever is to survive the paper war must learn how to be a decision-maker and not remain a paper-shuffler. Track every paper before leaving for the day. If there's a staff meeting immediately after school, make the unfinished sorting first on the following day's agenda.

TACKLE THE "TO DO" PILE

Set aside a regular time—every day or at least three times a week—when you can reasonably expect not to be interrupted. Try to find a time when students are not present. Fill out the requests for supplies, write the letter to Susie's mother, count the books for the inventory sheet, and record in your plan book the date and time of the next grade level meeting and the staff Christmas party. Make a note to yourself to call the nearby college for a catalogue of new semester courses. As you go through the folder of things to do, keep an alert eye open for jobs that can be delegated to someone else. The secretary would probably be glad to fill out a form for you to attend the reading conference next month. Your aide will no doubt have time tomorrow to collect and prepare for shipping the supplementary books that are due in the central textbook office. When you delegate everything delegatable you are not trying to shirk your responsibilities, you are simply trying to survive.

In this stack of papers there probably will be something from the principal, the P.T.A., or the counselor to send home to parents. Distributing these papers is a job that someone else can do easily. It's an ideal job for a student. Mailboxes made of half-gallon milk cartons or round ice-cream containers make convenient places for papers that should go home. Keep your eyes open for a permanent cabinet with mailbox cubby holes—it will save you the job of making new mailboxes each year. (Calloway House, Inc., 451 Richardson Drive, Lancaster, PA 17603 has an inexpensive "Message Center" with 36 separate compartments made of corrugated cardboard.)

If you find yourself repeating one type of paperwork with monotonous regularity, try thinking of more efficient ways to get it done. For example, your district may require that each parent sign a trip permit before students leave the school grounds on a field trip. Instead of doing this three times for three field trips, consider asking the administration to include in the enrollment package a trip permission slip that would cover the total year.

If you like to keep close communication going between school and home but find yourself spending many minutes every day writing letters to parents or individual children, consider making ditto copies of notes that say, "_____ has excelled in _____ [subject] this week. Ask to hear about it," or "Today has been a _____ [good day, bad day] for _____ . Ask to hear about it, then please sign this note and return it." Presigned, these notes are ready to go in a flash!

If this seems less personal than you like, save yourself at least some time by using a small sheet of paper, forcing you to keep the note short. Used computer cards or post cards are just the right size for this.

DEVISE A FILING SYSTEM

Decide carefully what labels you'll use. Broad categories serve best. Most successful filing systems follow strict alphabetical order without subgroupings. Don't place a folder labeled "Books—New," behind a folder labeled "Reading." Instead, place it alphabetically under "Books" and eliminate the need to remember both the major heading and a subheading.

Use simple categories. A folder labeled "Math Games" is far more useful and accessible than three folders labeled "Bingo," "Measure Up," and "Spin to Win." Avoid making a "Miscellaneous" file. It's no better than having a stack of papers on your desk.

In addition to a general file, some teachers find it helpful to establish a separate subject-matter file for each major curriculum area—math, reading, science, social studies, and spelling.

Behind each major heading go folders for such things as pretests, supplementary books, art projects, dittos, and the like.

Instead of a subject-matter system you might prefer a month-by-month one. Place those things needed in September, in October, and so forth in files labeled with month names.

Whatever filing plan you come up with, keep it simple and consistent so you won't waste time trying to remember where you've put something.

FILE THEM

If you have done your sorting well, the "To File" folder should contain only those important items you really want to keep. You should be certain that sometime in the near future you will want to take each paper out and use it in one way or another.

If you can't decide between two headings for a paper, put it in one folder and drop a note in the other for cross-reference.

Don't file entire magazines or bulletins. Clip those articles you want to keep and throw away the rest.

THIN THEM OUT

It's a good idea to keep your files appropriately trim and up to date by thinning them out from time to time by pulling and discarding what's out of date or what now lacks the freshness it had for you when you first filed it. A continuous process of updating works best. Each time you file new material go through certain files — A through E, F through M, September through November, and so forth — and remove what you no longer need. If it's too much work to weed every time you file, do it every other time, or once a week, or once a month. Whatever your schedule, update your files regularly.

CLASSROOM PAPERS

Part of the everyday routine of most classrooms includes written assignments. Some of these assignments are designed to provide practice to help assimilate and retain learning. Some papers serve to demonstrate knowledge, so that teachers can decide what needs to be retaught, modified, or extended. Some assignments provide opportunities for students to express themselves creatively. These and other types of written assignments will number, during the course of a year, in the hundreds, if not thousands.

Correcting all these papers for a roomful of students creates, as every teacher knows, a time-consuming job for someone. Since time is limited, and time spent doing one thing cannot also be used doing something else, teachers must take care not to be overwhelmed by correcting papers. The purposes of specific assignments, the age of the students, the people available to help with class routines, and your educational philosophy, among other things, will all bear on decisions you make about correcting papers. The following Shortcuts address pedagogical concerns as well as routine details in suggesting ways to lighten your correcting load.

✄ SHORTCUTS

DON'T CORRECT THEM ALL

With no feelings of guilt, you can collect many papers from students and simply throw them away. Practice assignments should be treated as just that, opportunities for students to practice. Of course you should be very active during these assignmnents—circulating among the students, identifying errors, reteaching on the spot, and seeing that corrections are made immediately.

B. F. Skinner's behavioral experiments should have convinced us long ago that the sooner errors are ascertained and corrected, the more likely it is that sound and lasting learning will take place. The common procedure—the children hand in assignments; the teacher takes the papers home to correct and returns them to students the following day with the errors boldly marked in red ink and a grade summarized at the top of the page with "Very Good" or "7/12"—is contrary to good learning principles and a sinful waste of teacher time. If a mark pleases the student, the paper will probably make it home. If a mark is poor, chances are the paper will end up in some ditch or wastebasket, unexamined by anyone. Either way, students will not be learning from their practice. The most unfortunate part of this procedure is that students may have learned the wrong things and no one follows through to help them correct their errors. Before accurate learning can take place, children must unlearn what is learned in error. Papers collected after careful, on-the-spot checking can very well be thrown away, discreetly of course. Use the time you save in more productive ways. Save your aide time, too. Rather than putting volunteers or aides to work grading countless papers, which then get put in student mailboxes to be taken home or ignored, train that aide or volunteer to work directly with students.

SPOT-CHECK PAPERS

It is human nature to want to have some recognition for effort put forth. Children's motivation to work will weaken if some reinforcement is not given at least intermittently. As students are working, the teacher can quickly assess a whole series of papers at each student's desk and mark them with stars, happy faces, "Well done," and so forth. Doing this kind of checking, you're not so much interested in finding careless mistakes as in ascertaining whether or not students have a basic understanding of the material the assignment covers. Reading three comprehension answers out of the ten assigned will give you a fair idea whether or not the student is reading carefully and understands. Looking at one math problem per row, a whole row at the end, three or four problems at random (and switching often so that students will not be able to outsmart the system) provides a good indication of students' mastery of operations and concepts. To do another kind of spot-checking have students complete practice sheets, but don't correct them. Instead write three new problems on the board, ones that require understanding the concepts they're working on. Have the students do these new problems, which you will check.

One teacher explains a "code" to parents at the beginning of each school year. Any paper with a general evaluative statement, such as "Excellent," has been spot-checked, but all errors may not have been caught. If a paper shows numbers such as "9/10" (nine out of ten items correctly done), the assignment has been carefully checked and the grade recorded.

LET CHILDREN CHECK EACH OTHER

To save yourself the time it takes to make a key for a page of arithmetic problems or a reading comprehension test, let the first three children finished go outside the classroom door, compare their answers, and decide upon a consensus of right answers, or "key." If their answers differ, instruct them to rework the disputed problems separately until there is agreement. Then they can return to the classroom and serve as checkers for the rest of the class.

MAKE PAPERS EASY TO CHECK

Make the tests and assignments that you will check completely as easy to correct as possible. Put problems or questions in straight, uniform rows so that the answers on the key can be placed directly next to answers on student papers and folded for succeeding rows. Another method is to make a place for answers along the right-hand side of a worksheet. Students will do the exercises on other parts of the page as usual, but will record answers in the side column. This makes for quick checking for accuracy and also allows for analysis of errors because the student's work is on the same page.

LET CHILDREN CHECK THEIR OWN

When you expend energy and time to do something, it's nice to know if you're doing it right. Nowhere is this principle more relevant than with your students. They progress fastest with frequent reinforcement and immediate feedback. Allowing children to correct some of their own papers can be a very positive procedure as well as a time-saver. Work done in centers, timed math tests, reading workbooks, and spelling practice tests all lend themselves to self-correction. Students can answer questions at the ends of chapters in health, science, or social studies books and then check them for correctness by rereading the chapter. You can write answers on the board and read them aloud for group self-correction. (Students can correct their own papers or exchange them with classmates.) Take considerable care to instill the idea that cheating during this process hurts no one except the cheater.

As always, there needs to be some provision for students to correct errors. Make dismissal for recess or home dependent upon the correction of wrong answers. Or, send papers home to be returned the following day with errors corrected (and perhaps signed by the parents). Those with papers to take home should write their names on the chalkboard; when they return their papers they can erase their names.

RECORD-KEEPING

Although there is no firm evidence that an increase in record-keeping results in an incease in learning, there is much documented proof that successful experiences in the classroom are clearly related to achievement. Common sense tells us that the more teachers know about each student under their supervision, the better able they will be to design successful experiences for those students. The problem, then, is keeping track of what each child has learned and is ready to learn next. It should be clear that the most important reasons for teachers to keep records is to aid lesson planning. Specialists who work with students also need information about students for the same reason.

AN OPEN BOOK

Keeping records that students can interpret and apply themselves and making such records available to them is an essential part of a teacher's job. Records help stimulate continued and greater efforts. A knowledge of one's progress can serve to increase a desire for improvement. Records supply students with the information they need to set goals for themselves and to develop a realistic view of their own abilities.

Parents and administrators need concrete evidence of a student's strengths and weaknesses to give both the student and his or her teacher the help and support they need. Principals also need some way of verifying that mandatory material is being covered.

Teachers need to supply school funding agencies with proof of each student's progress. As school funding by state and federal governments increases, the demands for accountability will continue to increase as well. If records are to form the basis for obtaining the funds that teachers need to run their classrooms, then it makes sense to keep them.

Teachers, specialists, students, parents, administrators and funding agencies all have a need for records. The problem facing the teacher, then, is to try to devise a system for keeping records that will meet the demands of those who use them and be as painless as possible to set up and maintain.

In most schools and districts across the nation teachers are locked into specific recording systems. The following Shortcuts fit into two categories—those that apply to the most common systems and those that will be useful to teachers fortunate enough to be able to choose and set up their own methods.

✂ *SHORTCUTS*

LET ONE CHART DO MOST OF THE JOB

If you must keep pupil profile records covering district or state continuums, put all the required information on one large chart or on the inside of a single legal-sized file folder (use both sides inside). It is easier and faster to record information for the whole class on a single chart than it is to make entries on individual folders. Don't duplicate information; keep it one place only. A chart is more useful for teaching; one glance can locate common weaknesses or pinpoint the next concept to be covered.

The chart shown on the next page works well for keeping track of student progress. Construct it in two parts. First, get graph paper

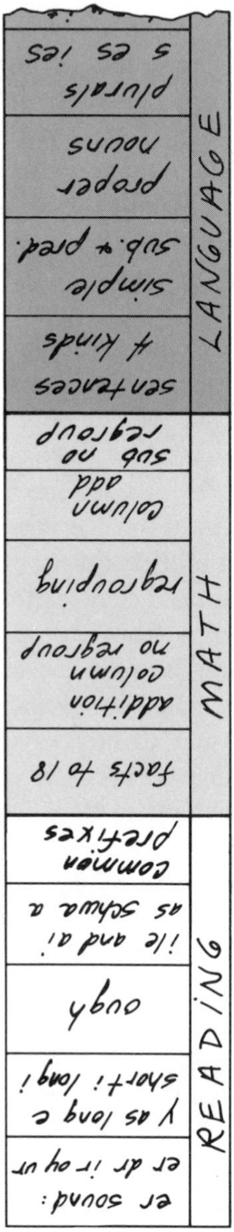

Permanent Heading Strip

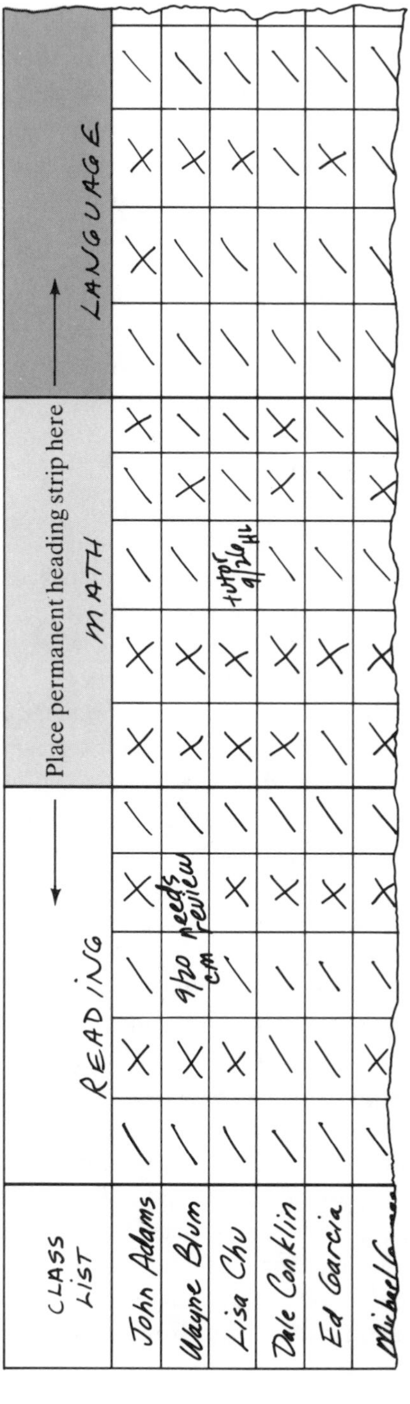

Student Progress Chart

with enough space to enter all your students' names down the side and all the continuum items along the top. Glue the graph paper to a piece of tagboard and fill in students' names at the left, as shown. Then cut a narrow strip of tagboard the width of your chart and divide it into sections the same width as the squares on the graph paper. List continuum items on it as shown. Don't list all items; combine those that obviously go together. Color code by subject area for quick reference. See "Simplify the Continuum," page 65, for examples of how to do this. Laminate the strip, tape it in place at the top of your chart, and you're ready to go. At the beginning of the next year, you can remove the strip and use it on a new chart for your new class. Put the chart on the inside of a cupboard door where it will be easy to keep up to date and easy for others to consult. If you prefer to keep it on the inside of a single legal-sized file folder, keep it in the very front of a file drawer, handy for everyone.

Most continuum or subject matter pupil profile records call for a slash (/) when a concept has been introduced and a cross (X) when the student has accomplished it. Immediately slash all those items that you know you will be working on during the year. Experience has shown that you will need to teach, reteach, and review these concepts all year. Delay changing the slashes to crosses on the profile records until near the end of the year when you are certain that what students have learned is likely to be retained. Be careful not to merely pretest, teach a concept (enter a slash), posttest (if passed enter a cross), then forget the concept and move on to the next one. Some teachers become preoccupied with these profiles. Because their districts recommend their use, teachers believe they are to move ahead, letting the continuum lead the way. If you ignore the need for periodic reviews and do not reteach, you may find that forgetting has outdistanced learning. Most elementary students can pass the posttest right after a concept has been taught but will have forgotten in a few days. If someone questions you about your profiles and implies that you are not keeping them up to date, explain that learning has been inconsistent and you are reteaching periodically to ensure mastery. Make your entries only two or three times a year. Ask your specialists to make notes right on the chart. Making and marking this chart takes very little time. It gives you a handy guide to the direction of your class, and administrators and funding agencies will find it reassuring.

RECORD THE LAST ONE ONLY

If your school is using a workbook series with a built-in testing program that follows your texts, recommend that only the last workbook test booklet completed for the year be corrected and recorded for the receiving teacher's benefit. This does not mean you will ignore the earlier skill test booklets. You can quickly glance at the work in them noting for your own planning problem areas and weaknesses. But you can omit correcting and recording every booklet except the last.

BUILD RECORD-KEEPING INTO
YOUR REGULAR TEACHING ROUTINE

Keep records on school time, during lessons. For example, if your students write in journals or books daily, spend 20 minutes on input as you go from desk to desk to help with words and so forth. Spend the remaining time with a few students, one at a time, and check on the previous five days' writing. Record on the back of the journal what you and each student understand as weaknesses to be worked on or strengths to be developed. Initial and date your entry and the bottom corner of the last page checked. The next time you work with a particular student you will only have to check those pages coming after your last initial. If you work with just seven students a day, you will be able to cover an entire class in a week.

For series of tasks you want your class to work their way through, number the tasks and make a ditto master with each task number written on it. Run enough dittos for each student, and when a student has completed a task, go over it with him or her. If the student has learned the concept, initial and date the appropriate number and write any comments beside it while the student watches. Note weaknesses and tasks to be repeated. For instance, if task number 20 still needs work, mark it with an asterisk or a triangle and write "Redo #20" in the margin. When the student finally masters number 20, date and initial it.

RECORD SUPPLEMENTARY READING
AS IT'S DONE

For a record of students' supplementary reading, separate available books into subject areas (dogs, cars, mysteries), reading levels (Primer, Level 1, Level 2), or by series. Put each group of books into a separate ice-cream bucket or cardboard carton. Ditto a separate reading record for each group and list the books it contains. Run enough for each student to have one copy in each carton. If you have 10 cartons and 35 students, you will need to run 350 copies, but these will take care of an entire year. In each carton keep sheets in folders. A student who reads a book from a carton will bring you a sheet from that carton when he or she has finished reading the book. You will ask questions, listen to some of it read orally, and so forth. Then write your comments on the sheet with the date, after which the student will refile the sheet. This procedure keeps you in touch with student interests, number of books read, comprehension, vocabulary mastery, and so forth. It also allows you to control level, variety, and skills. The record is made on school time, during lessons; it takes only a few seconds to evaluate reading and make entries. On those days when you are caught without enough time for regular lesson planning, or when students need a change, have a ''Bucket Book Day'' and let the entire class read from the cartons. You will only have to check their progress and make notes on your observations as they complete books. It's an easy day for everyone.

MAKE CHARTS FOR WORKBOOKS

With the right system and some advance preparation, you can simply, quickly, and efficiently record students' work in all the various workbooks now used in most classrooms. The records you keep can tell you and your students at a glance where they are, can inform parents of their children's progress, and can help administrators and evaluating teams get a profile of your class. Here is a simple way to make a record of students' progress in workbooks:

1. On a dittomaster, make a chart (8½ x 11 inches) with 10 rows of 10 squares each, numbered 1–100. On a second master, make an identical chart, this one numbered 101– 200. The numbers in the squares correspond to workbook page numbers.

2. Ditto enough sheets for each student to have a chart for each workbook he or she will use during the year.

3. Each student can make his or her own workbook record, or parent volunteers or older students can make them. First, glue record sheets onto pieces of 9 x 12 inch colored con-

struction paper. Each workbook will have a different colored page — math, red; reading, bue; spelling, orange; and so forth. Workbooks with 100 or fewer pages will need one chart, 1–100, glued to the front of the construction paper page; those with more than 100 pages will need two charts, 1–100 and 101–200, glued to the front and the back of the construction paper page.

4. When the pages are all prepared, add tagboard or construction paper covers and make books using a hole punch and brass brads.

These same records can be used in place of continuum records if workbooks have an official place in your school-site programs. Using the teacher's guide index that accompanies the workbook and breaks the work into skills and page numbers, color-code your own copy of the number sheets accordingly. For example, if pages 1–10 are devoted to numeration, color those numbers on your record sheet red; if pages 11–19 are operations, color them a different color; and so forth until most of the items on your continuum are accounted for in the workbook. If more than one concept is covered on a single page, divide the numbered square and color code the halves. This colored ditto copy is your "key" sheet. Once you have memorized the colors, a quick glance will tell you what is taught on a page. In our example on pages 70–71, we indicate various colors by using different patterns.

As students work in workbooks, move from desk to desk, teaching and spot-checking work as you go. When students finish a page, check for understanding; if the concept has been learned, initial and date the numbered square in the student's record book. If you are not satisfied draw a line around that square and do not initial it. The student will repeat the work, and you will initial the record when you are completely satisfied that the work on that page has been mastered. You can also mark the errors on the workbook page and allow students to make corrections before you initial the record. Using workbooks nonconsumably works well with this system. Simply have the students erase the plastic sleeve over the workbook page when they understand and have earned your initials on the record book. They then move on to the next page you assign.

In one walk around the room during a work period you can teach a concept, reteach where necessary, check work, hold the

Page Number Key for Workbooks

PLACE VALUE									
1	2	3	4	5	6	7	8	9	10
		ADDITION THROUGH 19							
11	12	13	14	15	16	17	18	19	20
21	22	23	24	25	26	27	28	29	30
CENTIMETERS				ADDITION		SUBTRACTION			
31	32	33	34	35	36	37	38	39	40
							PROBLEM SOLVING		
41	42	43	44	45	46	47	48	49	50
MULTI									
51	52	53	54	55	56	57	58	59	60
						CENTIMETERS			
61	62	63	64	65	66	67	68	69	70
GRAPHING						STORY PROBLEMS			
71	72	73	74	75	76	77	78	79	80
								TEMPERATURE	
81	82	83	84	85	86	87	88	89	90
TIME					MULTI				
91	92	93	94	95	96	97	98	99	100

= Numeration

= Operations

= Measurement

= Fractions

= Geometry

= Tests

Page Number Key for Workbooks

MULTI 101	102	103	104	105	106	107	108	109	110
111	112	PROBLEM SOLVING 113	114	115	116	117	118	119	120
121	122	123	124	125	126	127	128	129	130
LITERS 131	132	133	134	135	136	DIVISION 137	138	139	140
TRIANGLES 141	142	143	144	145	146	147	148	149	150
151	152	153	154	155	156	157	158	159	160
161	162	163	164	165	166	167	168	169	170
171	172	173	174	175	176	177	178	179	180
181	182	183	184	185	186	187	188	189	190
191	192	193	194	195	196	197	198	199	200

= Numeration

= Operations

= Measurement

= Fractions

= Geometry

= Tests

students accountable for correcting mistakes, make a record of students strengths and weaknesses, and provide a way for students to work at their own rate (individualizing). By referring to your key, you can also compile a record of where you and your students are in terms of continuum concepts.

Your students can work their way through a workbook beginning on page one if necessary. Or you can assign them work on various skills by referring to your color-coded key for page numbers. You save planning time and at the same time individualize your instruction.

If an administrator or an evaluation team requests information about one student, you can, with key in hand, turn to various pages in the student's record book and give a complete run-down in all the various academic areas. Having this information right at hand will increase your confidence. And with their own record books, students will be able to keep track of their progress and have a realistic picture of their strengths and weaknesses.

Train your aide, volunteers, cross-age tutors, and strong students in your class to help you run this system and make records for you. The guides that come with workbooks make giving directions and checking work simple. Asking students to explain what they did is an easy way to check understanding of concepts. Show your helpers how to initial and date both the worksheet and the student's record book. This system seems to be more accurate, is easier to use, and gives information more useful to teachers than those in many schools. If you are being inundated with demands for records at your school, it might be well worth your time to try this system and then attempt to convince your principal, school-improvement council, or district to accept it in lieu of those systems being used.

MAKE THE RECORDS YOU
KEEP MEANINGFUL

Knowing what each student does or does not do each day in the major academic areas is extremely useful information for a teacher to have. However, keeping records of all daily work can seem like such an impossible undertaking that few would attempt it. This Shortcut pares daily record-keeping down to manageable size. It involves making 5 x 8 inch record cards for each subject area. Each card has a student's name and enough space for two weeks' worth of marks. Record marks on these cards during lessons. Even though you'll need to make a new set of these cards every two weeks, the time you save trying to remember detailed information for recording after school and on weekends will be considerable.

1. On 5 x 8 inch cards, list all the students in your class down the left hand side—by group, by ability levels, or simply alphabetically.

2. Rule the cards into vertical, daily columns—M,T,W,Th,F. Try to fit at least 10 school days on each card.

3. Write subject titles and dates at the top of cards. Instead of making up cards individually each time, you might ditto a large number of charts, cut them to the 5 x 8 inch size, staple them to cards as needed, and fill in the appropriate subject titles and dates at the top.

4. Devise a very simple marking code that has meaning for you. For example if your card is for reading:

   □ Give a check (√) when you ask a student to read orally.

   □ Slash the check (X) if the student has difficulty (word reading, stumbling, lacking fluency, miscalling)

   □ Make an asterisk (*) when you ask a student a comprehension question.

   □ Circle the asterisk (⊛) if the student cannot answer the question correctly.

   □ Write any words the student misses in the daily square.

With these simple notes you have a record of words missed, comprehension skills, and general ability to read orally. You can see the whole group at a glance. Placing several of the two-week cards side by side in chronological order will reveal patterns in student work.

5. Keep these cards on a ring and you will have a daily performance record for each child for the entire year, a record made with very little effort while lessons were in progress. The benefit is that you need not expend any additional time compiling information.

Pupil Record Book Page

Spelling Workbook										
1	2	3 (DB 2/26)	4	5	6 (DB 3/1)	7	8	9	10	redo 8 ok
11	12	13	14	15	16	17 (DB 3/4)	18	19	20	missed 3 pg. 13 retest
21	22	23	24	25 →	26 make up	27	28	29	30	
31	32	33	34	35	36	37	38	39	40	
41	42	43	44	45	46	47	48	49	50	
51	52	53	54	55	56	57	58	59	60	
61	62	63	64	65	66	67	68	69	70	
71	72	73	74	75	76	77	78	79	80	
81	82	83	84	85	86	87	88	89	90	
91	92	93	94	95	96	97	98	99	100	

6. If you also write a simple description of what you taught each day at the top of each column, you will have a record of what skills were introduced and how well those skills were mastered.

If daily recording seems too much for you to attempt, do it only two or three days a week. Explain your system to your students if they are curious about what you are doing while they work. They may put forth greater effort once they know that what they do daily in your groups is important enough to record.

Suggest that, whenever possible, these daily performance records be used in lieu of additional teacher criterion-referenced test records. It is much easier to keep these notes daily or every few days than it is to give pretests and posttests, correct them, and record the results. And the information is far more meaningful.

LET OTHERS HELP

Train your aide, volunteers, school specialists, and students to help you keep records. If a helper or a specialist takes a student or group for tutoring or teaching, have that person make notes directly on your permanent records. There are some records, to be sure, that must be kept confidential, but most of the records kept at the classroom level are helpful only if everyone involved knows what they mean and how to update them.

Use your aides, tutors, and so forth to record and correct work completed. When they spot-check papers while students are working, have them initial and date the papers in a bottom corner. The same goes for individual student record books, pupil profile forms, or tracking sheets. Even student checkers can be trained to initial and date the appropriate square.

MAKE YOUR PLAN BOOK
A RECORD-KEEPER

What you put in your plan book is a legitimate record acceptable by state and federal evaluation agencies. Use it to save you time and effort. If 10, 15, or an entire unit of multicultural lessons are needed, suggest that the teachers in your school mark these lessons in their plan books so that additional records are not necessary. Whenever you teach an ethnic lesson, song, or dance; show a movie; introduce a speaker; or perform any class activity that meets multicultural requirements; circle the lesson in your plan book with an agreed-upon color. These plan books will be a record for evaluation teams or administrators who decide to verify your teaching. (For more on using plan books, see page 78.)

USE THE BEST–IT'S EASIEST

Most teachers would agree that dated samples of student work provide excellent, accurate records of academic growth. Unfortunately such records are difficult to box up to show to the legislators who allocate funds. However, if you work in a district that accepts such records as adequate, count yourself lucky and keep those papers with pleasure. Every two weeks, take a sample of work from a different subject area. First, reading; two weeks later, math; two weeks after that, language; and then repeat. On the prescribed day, have your students date their samples and file them in large file folders. Even kindergarten students can be taught to use a date stamp and to file their own work. Set up a large box so that file folders can hold art work and other large projects. If you color-code

the top portion of the folders, even very young students will be able
to find the right section and with a little training will learn to hold
the folders open so that papers do not get crumpled going in. Training takes time, but it pays off in time saved—you won't have to file
things yourself later.

WORK TO SAVE WORK

Volunteer to serve on the committee that writes or revises your
school's on-site programs. It is understandable that teachers consider these assignments just one more thing to do in an already
crowded schedule, but this is time that will save time and is therefore a good investment. When the writing of programs falls to those
who are not carrying a class workload, the paperwork and record-
keeping chores tend to grow considerably. Teacher know-how is
essential to a workable program. While serving on the program-
writing committee, let the Shortcuts in this chapter inspire you to
find ways to simplify record-keeping yet fullfill state and federal
mandates.

Some schools do not write their own programs and rely on the
district to determine what records will be needed for state and federal funding programs and what form the records must take. If you
work in such a district, volunteer to serve on the district-level committees that make these decisions. Serving for a few hours this year
may save you countless hours in subsequent years.

PLANNING

While it is true that the curriculum frameworks set up by federal, state, and district education departments make long-range, short-range, and daily planning a necessity, you don't need to devote huge amounts of time to making plans. With the right point of view and very little effort you can make planning a convenience, not an encumbrance.

THE PROCESS

To be an effective planner, you need to know the information in state and district frameworks or courses of study you will be using. You need to know what standardized tests or district proficiency levels will be used in judging students. You need to know which materials your school and district provide, which materials are available elsewhere, and what methods you will use for instruction (committees, lecture, individual research, and so forth). Also, you need to know who will be doing the work—teacher, tutor, or aide—as well as how much time guidelines say you must give to various subject areas.

Planning is essential to teaching because it demands that teachers think through what they're doing and where they're going. It is the thinking-through that is important, not the form of the written plan. Spend the bulk of your time thinking, not writing long, involved, detailed plans.

Though preparation and planning are really inseparable, for the sake of clarity and simplicity the discussion of how to get lesson materials and supplies ready ahead of time is in Chapter 3, beginning on page 47.

✂ SHORTCUTS

CENTRALIZE YOUR INFORMATION

It's important to put as much information as you can in one place where it is readily available. Let your plan book be that place. Use it as a calendar; take it to meetings and enter dates, deadlines, and pertinent notes directly into it. Use it at in-service meetings for notes of new ideas. Put parent conference appointments and abbreviated notes there, also. Adapt the pages in the front and back for as many uses as you can. Ignore the headings. Write on the front and back covers. You will be amazed at all the information your plan book will hold once you start trying to put everything in one place: volunteers' schedules, children's jobs, casts for plays, seating charts, aides' and volunteers' phone number and addresses, and so forth. ·

Don't succumb to suggestions found in guides and texts that tell you to abandon the plan book for a written form that gives you more room for detailed plans. Learn to write small and use one or two words to trigger the thinking that goes into your planning. As soon as details become part of established, routine procedures, leave them out altogether. Anything that becomes second nature, automatic, or part of your style should be left out—and that goes for all notes about materials or supplies that are regularly used.

Note all the tasks you are delegating to others in your daily lesson plan and let all your helpers know they can check the book whenever they need to. Train them to look there before they begin to work each day and especially before they ask you what to do. Underline volunteers' assignments with one color and your aide's with another so they can easily find their jobs for the day.

The front of your plan book is a good place to put all needed information from enrollment cards, such as addresses, phone numbers, birthdates, parents' work phone numbers, and so forth. Don't carry around a separate set of enrollment cards—they tend to get lost, out of order, and torn. Besides, once inscribed in your plan book, the information about your entire class is available at a glance on a single page.

LET STUDENTS HELP PLAN

When you use students as planners, you reduce your workload in two important ways. You plan on school time in a setting that makes other ideas readily available to you, and you improve motivation and discipline because student involvement ensures more interest and enthusiasm with less coercion. Using students when you plan obviously doesn't mean that students have the final say. You still retain the right to direct, delete, suggest, provide for flexibility, and set conditions.

Handing students a hefty book on day one and telling them that they will be expected to complete it by the end of the year can be a pretty discouraging start. Instead, tell students what must be done, but assure them that they can all help decide how the material will be covered, what the order of study will be, and what supplementary materials they'll use. Let them help with all phases of planning, beginning on the first day of school with long-range plans for the month, semester, or year. Record all their suggestions on the chalkboard or an extra large paper. Discuss everything. Don't spend time trying to be neat. Then pull from those long-range plans the information you need for short-range planning.

Going one step further, you can even use students as planners for the daily schedule if you make sure that they cover the basic requirements as well as special and extra time activities. A group of third-graders about to begin a unit on Hawaii could plan together how they'd like to proceed. Together they might discuss:

1. What are some of the things we'll need to know about Hawaii? (What Hawaiians eat, how they live, what they wear, how they have fun, and so forth)
2. How shall we organize outselves so we can learn these things? (Committee work, individual student reports, teacher lecture, other)

3. In what order shall we study the topics?

4. What materials shall we use to help us learn? (Films, filmstrips, guest speakers, books, encyclopedias, tapes)

Don't hesitate to use your students as planners just because you teach very young children. You may need to assume a slightly greater role, but with your guidance, even your very young students can, and should, help plan. Keep reminding yourself that learning results from mutual planning, and time-saving does too.

MAKE SOME PLANNING PERMANENT

When you find patterns appearing in your lessons (reading groups, for instance), identical lessons that need to be repeated (spelling rules), or multiple uses for certain procedural lessons (research steps), outline these lessons on cards and make them permanent. A card with the steps in long division can first serve as a lesson plan and later be a student-help chart. A small chart with the following elements, placed in the reading instruction area, can be a permanent reading lesson plan:

1. phonetic review
2. silent reading
3. oral reading
4. questions (main idea, interpretation)
5. discussion (author, style, story)

Having a few of these cards in convenient places is a help to volunteers or aides and eliminates the need for the teacher to give reminder lessons to helpers.

MAKE A LESSON-CARD FILE

Put lessons that have worked especially well on small cards and keep them in a file. In subsequent years you can take out a card and paper clip it to the appropriate daily page in your plan book. This saves your rewriting the same lesson every year. Make any comments or changes on the card before refiling to keep lessons up to date. Reuseable cards work well for small, successful units that you will teach more than once. For example, make a series of cards in sequence for a unit on reptiles. The first card might be ''observation,'' the next might be ''similarities,'' then ''differences,'' and so forth. In subsequent years you will have several weeks' lessons already done. Keep your lesson plans simple and short. Use trigger words for information you might forget.

PLAN ACTIVITIES FOR ABSORBING STRAY BITS OF TIME

Plan with students things they can do if they finish assignments ahead of time, if they earn independent time, or if your lessons run short. These activities are also good for the times when a visitor or an administrator drops into the room and needs your attention. Display these activity ideas on permanent plan cards available for all to consult. A math activity card might contain items like these:

1. Assign each letter in the alphabet a value:
   A B C D . . . . Z
   1 2 3 4 26
   a. Find the value of your name.
   b. What spelling word has the greatest value?
   c. Can you find a word with the value of exactly 50, 100, 150?
2. Skip count by 3 beginning at _____ .
   Skip count backwards by 6 beginning at _____ .
3. Make up _____ story problems about the class.
4. List 30 other names for 7. Example: $6 + 1, 49 \div 7$

A language activity chart might contain tasks similar to these:

1. Rewrite "The boy jumped into the pool," changing the nouns and the verb. Make 10 new sentences.
2. Using the letters in your own first and last names, make as many words as you can.
3. Make a list of as many opposites as you can (for example, up–down).
4. Using a page from your reader, write all the "sensory" words you can find. These are words that help you see, hear, or feel what is happening (for example, quietly, bright, shy).

GIVE UP GIMMICKS

Stop looking for things that will "turn students on" to your lessons. It isn't necessary to give each child a red balloon when you teach the

word red, to distribute apples when you read the story of Johnny
Appleseed, to make a puppet called "Timmy Cold Germ" for a
health lesson, or to manufacture a smoke-spewing volcano for a unit
on Hawaii. It requires a great deal of time and energy to devise,
make, and store such gimmicks. Your emphasis should be on the
satisfaction of learning new material rather than on superimposed
"fun."

Some lessons are clearly enhanced by extras. Let students supply them whenever it's practical. If apples, oranges, bananas and so
forth will really improve a lesson on types of fruit, ask students to
bring them in. If you can't do without puppets or volcanoes, have
students make them during art lessons or at home. And don't try to
save all the goodies for next year. Storing them is a hassle. Let the
next class make its own.

SIMPLIFY THE CONTINUUM

Eliminate some of the intermediate developmental items on district
and state continuums especially if they would naturally occur as
parts of other lessons. Many continuums are too cumbersome to use
effectively. Some have 40–70 entries in one subject area. Don't try
to plan lessons on each tiny step. Lump together those that go
together. For example, "rote count to 9,999; read a four-digit
number to 9,999; give place value to each digit in a four-digit
number; write numbers to 9,999; use comma in four-digit numbers;
compare a number to 9,999" can all be lumped for your purposes
into "read and write numbers 0–9,999." It is a rare teacher who
doesn't think in terms of task analysis, so those little steps will not
be ignored. Just be aware that detailed steps are there when you
need to consult them, and work with your own shortened version.

MAKE PERMANENT PLANS FOR
SUBSTITUTES

Even when they're not feeling well, many teachers somehow drag
themselves to school anyway—often against doctor's orders and
their own better judgment—just because it is too much trouble to
make plans for a substitute. Is there any other profession that requires one when ill to spend time trying to think through a day's
work for someone else; and if the illness has come on unexpectedly
in the night, trying to arrange for someone to take the plans to work?

Since even the healthiest of teachers can expect to be absent sometime, it pays to take some time at the beginning of the school year
arranging for an orderly, easy transfer of teaching duties to a substitute when it becomes necessary.

Begin by making a permanent record of your daily schedule in
your plan book, and make it detailed. For example:

8:35 Teacher reads with Green group; Mrs. Wilson comes on
Tuesday to read with Jon W.; aide reads with Red
group.

9:10 Teacher reads with Red group; ESL teacher takes José
and Mansy for 20 minutes each day; aide works with
Green group.

9:30 Balance of children arrive; children handle opening
ceremonies (Erica).

9:40 Spelling and language arts: Each child has consumable
workbook for spelling and a handwriting book in each
desk (Wed. library from 9:40–10:10).

10:10 Recess: We have permanent equipment monitors
(Susan, jump ropes; Fred, balls).

10:20 Math: Houghton Mifflin teacher's guide is on teacher's
desk with marker for place.

11:20 Prepare for lunch; aide handles lunch tickets.

11:25 Lunch: Wooden disk showing what cafeteria line we use
is on chalkboard rail.

12:15: Students rest while teacher reads from ongoing literature book (on teacher's desk marked for place).

12:30 Social Studies: Guides are on teacher's desk (Wed.,
health; Fri., science instead of social studies).

1:15 Uninterrupted silent sustained reading: The entire class
reads. Children have books in their desks. Allow first
three minutes for exchanging books they have finished
for new ones from bookshelf.

1:35 Physical education: Favorite games are dodge ball, re-
lays, and three deep.

2:10 Teacher reads with Blue group; Yellow group does assignment in workbook that follows up previous day's
lesson. Ask Gigi for details.

3:00 Dismissal

Notes: —The discipline code is on chart on west wall.

—If a child must be removed from the room, send to Room 18 with work.

—The seating plan is in front of plan book. "Good helpers" are circled in blue; those needing frequent reminders are circled in red.

—Teacher's lounge is in the middle of the adjacent building, south.

—Rainy day lunch hour is shortened by 10 minutes. Children return to room after finishing in cafeteria. They're supervised by noon play directors. Arrange for them to have at least one sheet of construction paper for art activity.

—Teachers' guides are on teacher's desk with colored markers showing current place. Some reading markers have names of children reading in that group.

—Thursday is an early day; all children come at 8:30 and are dismissed at 2:10. Use *Weekly Readers* for reading.

—Additional suggestions for activities will be found in top file drawer in the folder marked "Substitute."

Flag the page in your plan book where this basic daily schedule is kept with a label marked "Substitute." With this information, a substitute should be able to carry on a meaningful day in your absence with little additional information or effort from you. However, you may want to provide a second set of suggestions that can make the day run even smoother. These should be kept in your file in a "Substitutes" folder. Ditto enough copies to last the entire year; some substitutes may want to keep a copy for their own files.

The following ideas are appropriate for third or fourth grades. Adjust yours to fit your grade level.

IDEAS FOR SUBSTITUTES

Reading or Language Arts

1. Write five words on the board. Ask students to write a story using those words and then illustrate the story.

    Example: red   railroad   man   slippery   cloud

2. Ask students to make an alphabetical list of things that could be taken on a trip.

    Example: a-apple b-bedroll c-carrot d-dime

    Variations: Designate what kind of trip:

    to the mountains, to the city, to the seashore.

3. Ask students to write four sentences about events that could really happen, then to write four other sentences about impossible events. Say, "Make your spelling and punctuation the very best you can!"

Spelling

Have students write the spelling words using one of these variations:

1. Have students put them in alphabetical order.

2. Have students make as many new words as possible from the letters in each word.

    Example: From the spelling word *drink* you can make *in, ink, rink, kid, kin,* and *din.*

3. Have students "rainbow write" (trace over each spelling word with crayon beginning with the lighter colors such as yellow, orange, and ending with purple and black).

4. Have students group spelling words into classes. Example: *picture words:* desk apple.

doing words	*describing words*	*helping words*
running	pretty	the
think	fast	an

5. Have students write a story using as many words as possible from the spelling list. Say, "Every time you use one of this week's spelling words, underline it."

Social Studies

1. The teacher reads a chapter in social studies text wherever marker shows current place.

    a. Summarize the chapter with entire class and record their summaries on the chalkboard. The children copy and illustrate.

    b. Or, have students write their own stories telling about three things they have learned. Children then illustrate their stories.

2. Do a "recall" lesson reviewing what students have previously learned in unit. Ask them to:

    a. Draw one large picture showing as many facts as possible (at least five).

    b. List what they would see on a trip to the place being studied.

        Example: Hawaii—palm trees, sand, coconuts, pineapples, water, and so forth.

Math

1. Check marker in math teacher's guide to see what material has been studied. Write the following numbers on chalkboard:

$$12 \quad 34 \quad 56 \quad 78 \quad 90$$

If stuents have been studying multiplication have them multiply each number by 2, 3, and 4.

If subtraction: subtract each number from 100, 478, and so forth.

If addition: Add each number to itself. Add the first number to the second number, add that sum to the next number, and so forth.

2. Play Math Bug, a variation of the familiar game of Hangman. Choose a mathematical term, for example, *decimal*. Draw a picture of a "math bug" and place a dash for each of the letters in *decimal*. The children guess letters. If the letter is in the word, the teacher writes it in its proper place. If the letter is not in the word, erase one part of the bug. If the teacher erases the whole bug before students guess the word, the teacher wins. If the students guess the word and are able to give its definition before the bug is totally erased, the students win.

With these two sets of information for substitutes you should be able to stay home when you are not feeling well without making yourself feel worse. Remember, too, that "mental health days" taken now and then are Shortcuts when they send you back to work with a rested, fresh outlook.

DISCIPLINE

As a teacher you must devise some sort of discipline plan that ensures that your students behave in a manner conducive to a sound learning environment. All reports indicate that the number of discipline problems per class is increasing, that the kinds of discipline problems with which teachers must deal are becoming more difficult to solve (such as the increase in violent attacks upon teachers), and that large numbers of students with special problems are now being mainstreamed into regular classrooms. All this makes learning new control skills and establishing a well-formulated discipline plan imperative.

A DISCIPLINE SYSTEM FOR YOUR CLASSROOM

Classroom discipline is the subject of an ever-increasing body of information. Full-fledged, theoretically based, classroom-tested "how-to" systems (Assertive Discipline, Adlerian Psychology, Teacher Effectiveness, Behavior Modification, Glasser's Reality Therapy, and many others) are as close as your nearest bookstore,

library, or district consultants' offices. But before you adopt someone else's plan or revise your own, consider the following observations:

- ☐ You are solely responsible for leadership in your own
  classrooms. There must be a leader. If you do not assume
  that role, someone else, probably a student or several students, will assume it for you.
- ☐ School is basically an "enforced" situation. The students
  must be confined in a particular space for a certain length of
  time and must do things that they may or may not want to
  do. You also are locked into this "must be" and "must do"
  situation.
- ☐ You cannot always make school interesting nor can you
  always keep students from being bored. No one can.
- ☐ Your goal is to teach and to maintain an orderly environment in which students can learn. You cannot be all
  things—family counselor, substitute parent, psychologist—to all people.

This chapter does not seek to help you evaluate classroom
discipline systems or find one that perfectly suits your own needs.
You are the only person who can do that. Shop around, study,
carefully analyze various approaches. Take part of one system and
parts of others, and customize your own. If marbles and popcorn
parties are not right for you, don't use them. If rewarding every
instance of acceptable behavior is not something you care to do,
don't. Just because the teacher next door has had good results using
a particular method, you are not obliged to follow along.

However, experience has shown that it helps if all teachers in a
school agree on standards for student behavior and work towards
achieving those standards by whatever method suits each teacher
best. Establishing discipline then becomes a cooperative task, and
teachers' efforts reenforce each other. Further, establishing uniform
standards of behavior encourages teachers to share their own
methods of handling discipline and to borrow from each other those
techniques that seem to fit. Working together in establishing limits
of conduct has another advantage: it gives you some say in what
your fellow teachers do. Receiving a class of students from a lower
grade which has had little discipline the previous year means a
difficult time for the first few weeks of school. Teachers have an

obligation to one another not to make matters worse, and cooperative planning appears to be a solution to this problem.

Four words appear repeatedly in most books and articles on school discipline: *honest, fair, strict,* and *consistent.* In one form or another these four words seem to represent the basis of nearly all successful discipline systems. Important as they are, another word is even more important to the orderly conduct of students in your class: *caring.* Caring means watching over your students, paying serious attention to their needs, doing what needs to be done to respond to—if not always to fulfill—their needs, having a sincere interest in their concerns, and feeling a regard for them as worthy individuals. A caring teacher will automatically be more open, more honest about him or herself, less afraid to make mistakes and admit them to students. Such a teacher will receive their honesty in return. A caring teacher will be fair in dealing with students and impartial in applying rules. A caring teacher can be strict and still be considered fairer than a noncaring teacher, who might be judged mean for using an identical discipline technique. It takes a lot of caring always to follow through in a just and consistent manner when it would be so easy to let a problem go and save the bother.

Don't confuse caring with loving. Loving drains teacher energies; it's emotional involvement significantly different from and more intense than caring. Simply put, caring is the concerned yet respectful relationship needed for good discipline.

The following disciplinary Shortcuts are based on the assumption that you already have or will work out your own system of discipline; that you want to keep the importance of honesty, fairness, strictness, and consistency uppermost in mind as you shape your system; and that you are prepared to put the system to work in a caring manner. Some of the Shortcuts address tasks that you can shrink or eliminate to save time; others address the demeanor and attitudes that can save you enormous amounts of physical and psychological energy.

✂ SHORTCUTS

CONSIDER THIS
A SUGGESTED PLAN

You should read about several discipline systems and decide which one you prefer. But if you don't have time and if your district, unlike most, does not recommend a particular plan, you might want to try the following plan, which combines parts of several established systems, as a beginning.

1. Make classroom rules through discussion with students and put them on a permanent chart.

2. Follow discipline procedures consistently. For instance, write a student's name on the board for breaking one rule. That student will stay 10 minutes after school. Make a check beside the student's name for an additional infraction. That check means 20 minutes after school. Make a second check beside a student's name for a third. The second check means 30 minutes after school and an automatic phone call home.

3. For continued misconduct (a second day in a row with a triple penalty) have a conference with parent, teacher, and student present and send a note home daily for two weeks, to be signed by the parent and returned. The note should be very short (for example, Mary Jones, 1/14/80, ''good day'' or ''bad day'').

4. If the above steps don't prove effective, provide a cooling off period in the office or with a neighboring teacher. Provide work for the student to take along. Suggest a shortened day which is helpful if parents are not cooperative or don't follow through on notes sent home.

5. Turn to the principal for help or a referral to other support personnel—guidance counselor or psychologist.

Let your attitude toward rule breakers be one that says, ''You goofed, you made a mistake, now how can you make it right?'' Then have predetermined consequences that are fair, consistent, and based on the management system you use. In this way you provide your students with a chance to wipe the slate clean. If you do not follow through and instead leave the habitual disrupter with a guilty list of broken rules to carry from day to day, your job will increase as this student continues to consume your time with discipline. On the other hand, a student who has had to pay a penalty or write a new contract can erase his or her name or sign a new contract before leaving and come to school the following day with a sense of starting fresh. Your attitude should also be one of beginning anew with this student. The result will be fewer discipline problems and a lighter workload.

Protect the learning environment for the other children when a behavior problem is not solved by the above steps. Remove the recalcitrant student from the class for an extended period. A drastic measure is to have the student sit in the office at a desk away from the wall with absolutely nothing to do (nothing in pockets, no work, no conversation) for an entire week. After this punishment, the student usually is eager to go back to work in a classroom.

Give attention to other students for acceptable behavior and try to give attention and praise for every instance of good behavior on the part of the habitual disrupter.

PLAN RULES WITH STUDENTS

You will decide the steps to be taken, the procedures to be followed, and the consequences to be applied in your control management system, but you and your students together should formulate rules for conduct and decorum. Keep rules simple. Don't get into minute detail. You don't need five rules for exchanging papers or ten rules for bathroom conduct. Five or six rules covering classroom behavior should be sufficient. Examples of these general, broad rules are, "Raise hand before speaking," "Remain at desks unless given permission to leave," "Keep hands and feet to oneself," and so forth. Avoid vague rules. The directive "be good" in the auditorium does not set limits on conduct or establish standards to live up to unless all students know what "good" means — "Keep feet down on the floor," "Keep hands in lap," "Sit back in seats." In much the same way, you need to spell out what being "thoughtful" of others means. Rules should reflect the underlying organization you and your class need to maintain: "Stop working and clean up when the signal is given," "Be silent when the no talking sign is up," "Leave centers neat and clean."

Whatever the system, students need to know what specific behavior is expected of them, and they should take part in defining those expectations. When rules come from students, adhering to those rules becomes more a choice, less a dictate. The element of choice encourages greater cooperation and right away you have a discipline Shortcut. Write rules on a chart or ditto immediately, as they are decided. Do not wait to write them out later on your own time. Giving students a printed copy, putting rules on permanent display charts, and sending copies to parents to sign and return are all ideas you might want to consider if you think they can help reduce the time and effort you'll need to spend on classroom discipline.

DON'T MAKE THEM "YOUR" RULES

Keep in mind that class and school rules are not the personal possessions of teachers, so don't insist that students apologize to you or other teachers for breaking rules. Demanding and obtaining apologies requires too much energy and effort and just adds one more thing on which you must follow through. Spend your energies upholding natural consequences of misbehavior, not imposing artificial politeness. Of course, apologies are clearly in order when a student has insulted or hurt someone, disturbed another class, destroyed the work of another student, or committed some similar act. Teaching a few law-related lessons is time well spent when it helps everyone better understand the relationship between rules, enforcement, and consequences.

MAKE THE CONSEQUENCES FIT

Be sure that when a natural consequence is obvious, such as washing scribbles off the wall, you enforce that consequence instead of applying an unrelated consequence, such as 10 minutes with head down after school. Ten minutes scrubbing makes more sense than writing, "I will not scribble on the walls."

As a rule, consequences for misconduct should be determined by teachers because they need flexibility in applying natural consequences that fit the situation. A student who disrupts a lesson and has to be sent away from the group can stay ten minutes after school to do the work missed rather than sitting with head down or being sent to the office.

ELIMINATE CHECK-UPS AND FOLLOW-THROUGHS

When students don't comply with class rules and break their contracts, infringe upon the rights of others, refuse responsibility for their own fair choices, and so forth, they must pay the penalty your discipline system calls for. When students don't pay the necessary penalty, then noncompliance becomes an additional problem for you to deal with. For example, if a child does not stay after school or appear for an interview with the teacher after he or she disrupts a study period, you have to handle this non-compliance as well as the original infraction of the rules.

Look for ways of dealing with noncompliance that do not require even more of your attention. An automatic doubling of time after school, an automatic second checkmark beside a student's name on the board, or an automatic interview with the principal are added consequences that have worked for some teachers. If your system requires a record of the interview, of the rule broken, or of the penalty paid, devise a way students can keep records for you. For example, if a child is staying after school for 10 minutes, set a timer and go on with your own work. When the timer bell goes off, look up and nod to the student, who then may erase his or her own name from the board and enter his or her name in a record book with an abbreviated record of the rule broken (''T'' for talking, for instance). You do not need to leave your work, and you can quickly glance at the record book daily to see that entries were made correctly. Don't use your own time to write detailed contracts and lengthy anecdotal memos for a discipline system. Find a way to make this a student responsibility. Make a check list students can mark or devise a form that even young students can fill in.

Sample Form #1

CONTRACT

Name _____ Date _____

What did you do?

    1. Acted in an unsafe way _____

    2. Disturbed others _____

    3. Stole or destroyed property _____

    4. Disobeyed _____

    5. Was rude or insulting _____

    6. Other _____

         _____

         _____

What is your plan?

1. Try words to solve problems _____
2. Follow rules of games _____
3. Use equipment safely _____
4. Respect the rights of others _____
5. Obey adults _____
6. Use respectful language _____
7. Consider the rights of others _____
8. Other _____
   _____
   _____

Sample Form #2

Name _____ Date _____ Room No. _____

Had problem with:

manners _____	classroom rules _____
language _____	equipment _____
playground rules _____	fighting _____

Penalty _____
Follow through: teacher ☐   principal ☐   note home ☐

Do only what you must to maintain your leadership. Remember that it is less work to glance at something a student has written or filled out than it is to record information yourself.

DON'T LISTEN TO EXCUSES

When a student breaks a rule, don't listen to excuses. Put the system into effect, but in those cases where the system doesn't seem to fit, have the student write answers to these two questions: "What is the problem?" "What is your plan for solving it?" Later he or she can finish the record by answering: "Are you using the plan?" "Is it working?" You are saving the time you would have had to spend listening, the time you would have had to spend solving the problem, and you may also have decreased your discipline problems by not giving the rule breaker the attention he or she desired but didn't deserve.

REMOVE TEMPTATIONS

Remove temptations wherever possible. For example, devise a system for dealing with lunch money and personal belongings that cuts stealing to a minimum. You might have students place their money in large envelopes with their names on them, paperclip them closed, and keep the envelopes in their own mailboxes in full view of the class at all times. Taking the envelope out, unclipping it, removing the money, and putting the envelope back would be impossible without someone noticing; stashing the envelope somewhere would be equally difficult.

Putting a monitor on duty in the coatroom at strategic times, arranging the room so that the coatroom is in view, or making the coatroom off-limits unless the teacher or monitor is present can reduce the opportunites for mischief and theft.

IDENTIFY POTENTIAL PROBLEMS

If students get fidgety at certain times during your lessons, change the pace. Tighten things up and add more structure or slow things down and provide a time for conversing. Speeding things up can recapture attention, and giving a breather can renew interest. Make note of which lessons are dreary and need extra planning. Don't dismiss a fidgety class early. Students will catch on quickly, and soon you will have an epidemic of squirming.

STREAMLINE TRANSITIONS

Make transitions from one lesson to another simple, smooth, and habitual. Don't let putting-away and getting-out times drag out or be loose. Clumsy transitions not only waste time but also affect the quality of following lessons. When time requires that you stop an interesting lesson or project, give a few minutes notice and promise to plan extra time for those who need or want to work on it again. Keep your promise. You'll eliminate most moans and groans as well as discipline problems with those who refuse to stop right away.

RESPOND APPROPRIATELY TO RESTLESSNESS

When a class becomes restless and noisy, take a breather. Practice yoga or other relaxation methods for just a few minutes. Have some appropriate music handy for these times and train your class in progressive muscle relaxation, deep breathing, and visualization.

You will avoid problems if you don't misjudge general unrest and try to discipline large numbers of tired students.

DON'T BE THE ARBITRATOR

Let students settle everything they can by themselves. If two students in your room argue with one another, separate them from the rest of the class, put them in a specified place, tell them to reach an agreement, and ask them to bring it to you in writing in five minutes. Don't spend your time listening to both sides of such arguments and trying to solve the problem so that everyone wins.

If one of your students has a dispute with a student from another class, tell them that neither teacher will take action until they agree on what actually happened and then tell you how they should have handled the situation. Setting a common goal for them to reach in five minutes will usually eliminate the accusations and denials that are so time-consuming. Sending both students to the office with orders to reach an agreement before they get there will often result in a solution in two minutes flat.

GIVE EVERY STUDENT AN EQUAL CHANCE

To be most effective in administering a system of discipline, you must be fair and impartial in all areas—handing out special jobs, assigning students to teams or committees, and naming those who may go first. This Shortcut provides ways for you to build student confidence in your fairness, to eliminate resentment, and to create a positive classroom climate.

Number small pieces of paper from 1–35 (one for each student in your room) and put them into a bowl. Let each student pick a number (record who chose each number). When you need a special job done (one not covered by permanent job assignments), pull a number from the bowl and the student assigned that number for the month gets to run it. Better yet, let the students pull the numbers out. This makes the teacher an impartial participant. In setting up teams or committees, put numbers 1–8 on one team, 9–17 on team two, or draw numbers out of the bowl for each position on a team (number one is pitcher, number two is catcher, and so on). When you have students line up, ask numbers 1–5 to go first, 6–10 next, and so on. Notice that this system applies for special jobs and events, not the permanent classroom assignments mentioned in the chart "Managing the Classroom," page 17.

CONCENTRATE ON THE POSITIVE

Give verbal praise often for good conduct. It saves time. Telling students when you like what they are doing reinforces behavior you want to continue and thus cuts down on disciplinary interruptions.

Be sure when you praise or thank students, however, that compliments and pats on the back are well deserved. Don't give recognition and rewards indiscriminately. They lose their meaning and work against you. Unearned praise makes students uneasy.

Have students recognize the good things about themselves through writing, discussions, and rewards. Use the high correlation between good behavior and good self-image to cut your workload. The following are some things you might do on class time to enhance student self-concepts:

☐ Interview one student. Let the class ask questions and appoint one or two students to use the information obtained to write a story about the student. Teachers of younger students will have to do the writing, but even kindergarten students can learn to ask good questions. Feature this student on a chart or a news bulletin. Later let the student interview the class and see how much they remember about him or her.

☐ Make a big deal out of birthdays. Make crowns, sing songs, give special privileges, write a message on the board, let the class make cards. The last day of school can be "birthday" for summer birthdates.

☐ Have regular opportunities for sharing hobbies, pets, talents, favorite books, and so forth.

☐ Take informal snapshots of each child in your class. Hang the snapshots on a "People Tree" and write complimentary captions under each one.

☐ Interview parents of students for career planning units or whenever a parent's job fits in with what you're doing in class.

GIVE SIMPLE REWARDS

It isn't necessary to make elaborate rewards, such as felt badges, cut-outs, cute bookmarks, and the like, or buy candy or treasures with your own money. Look for other ways to accomplish the same end. If, for example, your students learn to receive recognition by

having their names written in a "Good Box" on the chalkboard, and
if you make a big deal of writing their names there, it can be just as
effective as giving them treasures. Draw a huge happy face when
you are pleased with a quiet study period or write "You were
great!" in giant letters after a fire drill in which your class performed well.

There are other simple rewards that fit many occasions, take
almost no teacher effort, and require no expenditure of teacher
funds. You can give free time to do a favorite class activity or allow
"winners" to eat lunch with you one lunch period a month. A
friendly chat with the principal is a good reward; most principals see
only problems and seem to welcome chances for positive contact.
Give "perfect citizens" the right to watch a special movie or invite
them to write their names on a "Good Citizens of the Month" chart
in the hall. Use ceremony to accomplish your objective, not time
and money.

USE BODY LANGUAGE

Learn to use body language; it is time saving and energy conserving.
Hand things to students with no comment, learn to lift an eyebrow,
frown a warning, smile a reward, lift a hand for silence. Most
teachers have developed these kinds of mannerisms, but they usually accompany them with words, probably believing that words and
gestures together are twice as effective. No so. Going to the board to
put a check beside a name without one word can be far more force-
ful than verbally chastising a student all the way there and back.
Students learn to tune out teachers who talk too much. Don't argue
or listen to excuses unless the system you have chosen demands it.
Just be certain you have the right offender and put your system
into effect.

USE YOUR VOICE EFFECTIVELY

Your voice is an effective tool. Use it to its fullest to dramatize, to
excite, to entice, to dispel, to disapprove, to reward, but don't use it
unnaturally. Some teachers, perhaps believing that soft voices calm
children down and teach them to listen closely, have developed
breathy whispers when they speak to the class. Others, believing
that low voices denote authority, have developed unnaturally deep
monotones. It takes a great deal of energy to whisper to a class all
day or to drive on in the lower octaves. Talking unnaturally in class

also seems a putdown to your students. They hear you talk one way to your fellow teachers and another way to them. They can't help but wonder why. This doesn't mean that whispers in a student's ear and a whispered private conversation with a student aren't good disciplinary techniques. It doesn't mean that a low monotone can't be effective. Just don't make the way you talk an affectation.

Neither should you yell. It saps your energy and emotions, undermines your prestige and credibility, and can cause damage to your vocal cords. Students may be shocked into silence the first time you yell "shut up," but it is rude and ineffective over the long run. Try a prearranged signal instead. Tap on the chalkboard with your chalk, clap a rhythm, raise one hand, write the word *SILENCE* in large letters on the board, or put out the lights.

EXPECT COMPLIANCE

When you make demands or give commands, let your manner convey the message that *of course* the student will comply. For example, tell a student who has scribbled on the hall walls that he or she will need to clean if off before leaving for the day and the cleanser is under the sink. Then turn and walk away and let your steps show that you are assuming the job will get done.

DON'T GIVE AWAY
YOUR EMOTIONAL ENERGIES

Keep your cool no matter what. Anger, frustration, and anxiety drain away energy you need for yourself. Emotional outbursts also steal your time. In this case, being selfish is a Shortcut. Be determined that no problem is worth that much to you. The key is having a discipline system that is well established, smooth-running, and as automatic as all the other procedures of the classroom. Carry through on discipline with a matter-of-fact, business-as-usual manner. Don't give any student the power to force you to overreact or to expend energy you need for yourself. Never chase a student who has broken a rule, even if fighting was involved and someone was hurt. Let the provisions of the system take over. Don't shake or swat a student. Legal or not, such actions rob you of strength, diminish student respect for your authority, and ultimately are likely to increase discipline problems. Don't let your own behavior increase your discipline workload. You cannot take discipline problems as personal affronts; let your system, not your emotions, rule.

TESTING

Endless debates are waged over the integrity of standardized tests. Many educators seriously question whether these tests actually work to measure pupil growth. Further, many complain that children spend more time being tested than being taught.

THE TEACHER'S ROLE

While the controversy continues, so does the use of standardized tests. Many school districts and state and federal agencies require them. It is the classroom teacher's task not only to administer the tests in a way that causes the least interference with regular work but also to do whatever he or she can to make sure that the results of a given test reveal as accurately as possible the actual abilities of each child tested.

Not all of the Shortcuts in this chapter are Shortcuts in the sense that they save teacher time and reduce workload. They are, however, Shortcuts to more accurate test scores.

✂ *SHORTCUTS*

ANALYZE YOUR ATTITUDE—IT SHOWS

Before children and a test are brought together, the teacher should be aware of the importance of his or her role in this encounter. The teacher's goes beyond actual academic instruction.

Children are very sensitive to their teachers' attitudes. Students will pick up teachers' negative feelings about tests. Negative attitudes increase the likelihood that test scores will be adversely affected. Sources of negative feelings abound:

- ☐ Teachers may feel that the test is a judgment of their own competency. They may be tense and grim and cause some students to freeze while taking the test.

- ☐ Teachers may have serious misgivings about the purpose and worth of the test. They will find it hard to convince students that "doing one's best" is worth the effort.

- ☐ Teachers may assume a cavalier attitude and not take the testing program seriously. Their students will likely assume a similar attitude.

It is bad for students to get the notion that their teacher is unsympathetic to a particular test. Regardless of a teacher's personal opinion about standardized tests, it is only fair to children that teachers try to make the best of the situation by assuming a positive attitude.

KNOW WHAT THE TEST IS MEASURING

The author of a test first attempts to establish what students can be normally expected to know at the time they take the test, then creates test items to measure knowledge or performance in relation to that norm. Teachers have the right to know what that norm is, or what a given test intends to measure.

Many districts make available to teachers synopses of areas that will be tested as well as sample exercises. Look for them and use them. Borrow the materials from a teacher friend from another district if your district doesn't have them. School counselors may be able to answer specific questions. Make notes for yourself if the same test is used each year. Then formulate your curriculum to make sure that when test time comes you and your students will be fairly evaluated.

Do not misunderstand: This Shortcut isn't advocating a "teach-to-the-test" curriculum. What it does advocate is a curriculum that will have included, during the course of the school year, most of the things on which students will be tested in the spring. It is woefully unfair to students and teachers alike to study one thing and be tested on another.

INFLUENCE STUDENT ATTITUDES

Since, in the final analysis, it is the student who takes the test, it follows that how that student feels about the whole procedure will affect the outcome. Too much fear and anxiety, too little concern or appreciation for the importance of the test, and not enough care in marking answers or following directions will produce an invalid test score.

There are children who suspect that, once collected, tests are thrown away—an understandable suspicion since students never see the tests again. Many children become extremely upset when they come across test questions they do not understand and are told not to ask the teacher for help. It's hardly surprising that they get upset because in all other situations the teacher has said, "Be sure to ask for help if you don't understand." The differentness and specialness of the standardized test situation should be brought out in the open and discussed with students. It is only in this way that erroneous assumptions can be rectified.

A unit on the nature of special tests should be part of the curriculum of every school child. Begin by explaining the purposes of the testing program to students. They should know that nearly all students take standardized tests almost every year they're in school. The tests are an important part of school and should be taken seriously. Though they may not see the tests again after finishing them, students should be assured that tests are indeed corrected and that scores are part of each student's permanent record. These records are available to principals, counselors, parents, and next year's teacher. The test scores are of such importance, however, that anyone outside of the school must get parent consent before being allowed to look at them. Inform students that decisions involving grade and class placement, tutoring opportunities, and chances for special help by specialists and others are made on the basis of test scores.

Finally, though a child deserves to know the importance that test scores can assume, he or she should also be assured that personal worth is not related to any test score. Teacher judgment will dictate whether or not students are shown their scores. The deciding question is, "Will it be helpful to the child to know?" Some teachers tell a child how many months' growth has been made between the pretest and posttest. Thus a child who remains below grade level but has made ten months' growth for seven months' instruction can still feel a sense of achievement. All that should be asked of students is that they do not cheat themselves by not putting forth full effort.

EXPLORE PROCEDURAL DIFFERENCES

Most children are accustomed to being tested almost daily in school. Teaching and testing are so much a part of classroom instruction that they are almost inseparable. However, tests that teachers use for information about student progress bear little resemblance to standardized tests. One major difference is the answer sheet. Explain to students that answer sheets are put through a special scoring machine to be corrected. The lead from the student's pencil used on the answer sheet triggers the machine to mark the answer either right or wrong. Using an answer sheet presents a new set of conditions that should be discussed with students. For example:

- ☐ Explore strategies for keeping one's place both in the test booklet and on the answer sheet.
- ☐ Discuss how answers can be changed. Students should know that they must erase thoroughly and completely.
- ☐ Alert students to the fact that only one answer should be marked for each question. Giving two answers to the same question, even though one answer is right, is an automatic error.
- ☐ Instruct students about the use of scratch paper, especially for math tests, since most test booklets cannot be written in. While the correct answer to some math problems should be obvious at a glance (often by eliminating choices that clearly cannot be right), others may demand more careful

calculation. Students should verify their chances by performing those calculations on scratch paper.

☐ Suggest that it is possible to do column addition, which can be a big time eater, without having to copy the problem on scratch paper. Tell them to put an edge of the scratch paper directly under the columns, add, and record numbers as in a standard column addition problem. The trick is to put the number to be carried at the bottom of the next column instead of the top (as shown below).

MAKE TIME WORK FOR THEM

Students may be accustomed to having as much time as they need to complete normal classroom tests. Standardized tests, on the other hand, are timed; a prescribed number of minutes is allotted to all students for the taking of the test. There will be no second chance, no few extra minutes to finish — ''Stop'' will mean ''Stop.'' Those students used to a more casual procedure need to be assured that there will be enough time to show what they know, if not finish the tests, if they use the time wisely. Remind them to:

☐ Start immediately.

☐ Work steadily. There is no time for daydreaming, looking out the window, thinking about last night's television show, and such. There is time enough occasionally to put down one's pencil, shake the cramps out of fingers, stretch necks, and flex shoulders. But, then it's back to work.

□ Resist the temptation to give any one problem or question an inordinate amount of time. Every test will contain questions that the student cannot answer or cannot answer quickly. Students can skip these questions temporarily and tackle them again after they've answered all those they're more certain of. Or they can answer with the best possible guess. Often a five-choice multiple answer can be narrowed to two or three reasonable possibilities, and one out of three "probables" makes for better odds than one out of five "possibles" guessed at. The significant point here is that no one question should take an inordinate amount of time.

□ Realize that these special tests may be longer than those they usually take. Thus forewarned, students are less likely to tire or to give up prematurely.

□ Read comprehension questions about a story or a paragraph first, then watch for the answers while reading the passage.

□ Listen carefully when directions are being given and ask questions at that time about anything that is not clear. Students should be helped to understand that special tests have special instructions, that the instructions are likely to vary from test to test, and that instructions are given at the beginning of the test only and cannot be repeated.

PREPARE THEM FOR
DIFFERENCES IN CONTENT

Teachers teach, then give criterion-referenced tests to see how much of what they have taught has been learned. If the lessons have been good and students have been attentive, their scores on such tests should be near the perfect mark. At the very least, students know there will be nothing on the tests that has not been taught. Not so with standardized tests. They include a wide range of questions, some relating to material that may not logically fall into the curriculum until some later time.

Explain that tests purposely contain a wide range of material. Some questions will be very easy and some will be very hard to answer. Warn students not to allow the hard questions to upset them. They should simply make a good guess and go on.

Further, explain that test items do not necessarily go from easy to harder to hardest. There is a tendency in that direction but there may be some questions that will be easy for them to answer at the very end of the test. They should keep looking for the easy questions throughout the test. This suggestion may counteract the temptation to quit after a couple of hard questions.

Finally, inform students that while taking standardized tests there will be no help from anyone. This facet of the testing program has been established so that the results will be fair for everyone.

GIVE THEM PRACTICE

To neutralize the possibility that unfamiliarity with the procedures of standardized testing will get in the way of valid evaluation, it seems prudent to provide practice throughout the year using a formal testing format. Give timed tests, use answer sheets, include questions that address material that hasn't been covered, make tests that are longer than normal, and so forth.

Providing a checklist for each student for self-evaluation of test-taking strategies may serve to improve test-taking skills.

Sample Test Checklist

Name _____ Date _____

Did I practice good test-taking habits by:

_____ 1. Listening to directions

_____ 2. Starting on time

_____ 3. Working steadily

_____ 4. Skipping or guessing those I did not know

_____ 5. Using scratch paper when necessary

_____ 6. Marking one answer for every question

I think I took this test

Poorly   Pretty Well   Really Well

GET THE MOST OUT OF TEST DAY

If there ever was a time for sound teacher judgment, test day is that time. Some classes may need a serious reminder of the importance of doing one's best. You can make a little speech:

This is ''opportunity'' day for you. You are being given the opportunity to show how much you've learned this year in math. Many people will be interested in the results, so I'm sure you won't want to embarrass yourself by not doing your best. That's all anyone asks—that you try hard. Remember, you aren't expected to know all the answers, so don't let that bother you; keep looking for ones you know. Good luck, I know you're going to do well.

Some classes may need to be relaxed with a joke, a smile, or a short speech:

You're have a special treat today. Instead of having to listen to me teach a math lesson, we're going to have a nice math test in a perfectly quiet room. That's got to be good news since I know you like to take tests better than listen to me. Relax, you're going to do well.

In either case, most classes will feel best about the whole procedure if their teacher administers the test, or at least is present in the room while they're taking the test. That way, he or she can circulate throughout the room giving a pat on the back where needed, a "you're doing well" whispered in an ear, a smile to one who looks about ready to give up. And, watch your voice. When giving directions make an effort to maintain a normal voice. Don't be too serious or unduly grave.

LET EVERYONE KNOW THE SCHEDULE

Ideally, all students will take the standardized tests on the scheduled days, the testing program will be finished, and classes will resume regular instructional patterns. However, the ideal is seldom the reality. Some children get sick, others play hooky, and still others stay home because grandmother is visiting. For whatever reasons, most teachers end the test-taking period with a stack of tests that have not been taken. Make-ups are a drain on someone's time, therefore anything a teacher can do to keep them to a minimum is a Shortcut.

Be sure the students know when a test is scheduled. And more importantly, let parents know. You may want to start early in the year enlisting parent cooperation for this at parent conferences or through newsletters such as the one shown below.

Dear Parent,

As part of the instructional program at Washington School, all children will be given standardized tests in October and again in May in the areas of language, reading, and math. This testing helps us assess your child's strengths and possible weaknesses so that we can provide instruction that will meet individual needs. Your child's teacher will let you know on exactly which days the tests will be given. We are sure you will want to see that your child is present and well rested for the tests so that the results will be an accurate record of his or her ability.

Thank you for your cooperation,

INFORM STUDENTS ABOUT MAKE-UPS

Tell children who may be thinking that test day is a good day to be absent that nothing short of evaporation from the face of the earth will release anyone from taking the test. Tell the class that absentees will be required to make up the test somewhere, sometime. The somewhere may be an isolated corner of the counselor's office, foyer of the auditorium, table in the cafeteria, or another classroom. The sometime may be during recess, before school, or after school. Although you should make it clear that the test is important, be careful not to make the test seem ominous. Putting too much emphasis on the test in this way may be counterproductive and serve to undermine students' confidence.

GET HELP GIVING MAKE-UPS

It might be possible for you and other teachers of the same grade to schedule standardized tests on different days. Thus, students who are absent on test day in one classroom might be able to take the test with another class. (Obviously this scheme won't help the teacher who has the last test day, except in the case of those students who know in advance they will be absent on test day.)

And don't forget to make use of other auxiliary people at your school for help with make-ups—specialists, counselors and their aides, vice-principals, and so forth. Try them all.